MUSIC BUSINESS
ESSENTIALS

MUSIC BUSINESS ESSENTIALS

A Guide for Aspiring Professionals

MARK CABANISS

Foreword by Mike Curb

ROWMAN & LITTLEFIELD
Lanham • Boulder • New York • London

Published by Rowman & Littlefield
An imprint of The Rowman & Littlefield Publishing Group, Inc.
4501 Forbes Boulevard, Suite 200, Lanham, Maryland 20706
www.rowman.com

Unit A, Whitacre Mews, 26-34 Stannary Street, London SE11 4AB

British Library Cataloguing in Publication Information Available

Library of Congress Cataloging-in-Publication Data

Names: Cabaniss, Mark, author.
Title: Music business essentials : a guide for aspiring professionals / Mark Cabaniss ;
    foreword by Mike Curb.
Description: Lanham : Rowman & Littlefield, 2018. | Includes bibliographical
    references and index.
Identifiers: LCCN 2018015296 (print) | LCCN 2018016094 (ebook) | ISBN
    9781442274556 (electronic) | ISBN 9781442274532 (cloth : alk. paper) |
    ISBN 9781442274549 (pbk. : alk. paper)
Subjects: LCSH: Music trade—Vocational guidance.
Classification: LCC ML3790 (ebook) | LCC ML3790 .C17 2018 (print) | DDC
780.68—dc23
LC record available at https://lccn.loc.gov/2018015296

∞™ The paper used in this publication meets the minimum requirements of
American National Standard for Information Sciences—Permanence of Paper
for Printed Library Materials, ANSI/NISO Z39.48-1992.

Printed in the United States of America

To all my students at
Belmont University . . . past, present, and future.

Thank you for teaching me and for the
honor and joy of teaching you.

CONTENTS

FOREWORD

I have been in the music industry for more than 50 years, and the many incredible changes to the industry have created a need for everyone who is part of this business to understand how those changes affect them. The delivery system has moved from vinyl records to cassettes to compact discs to downloads and now to streaming. The important thing, which has not changed, is the passion for music that ultimately allows the industry's participants to navigate through these changes. It is important to understand that a record, whether it's physical or digital, is ultimately what the consumer will relate to. Obviously, a record starts with a song. The method of recording, the choice of musicians, the interpretation of the recording artist, the musical arrangement, and the producer—who has the ultimate responsibility for bringing all these things together—all have an impact on the record.

Some artists need record labels more than others, but I have learned that it takes a lot of great people working in numerous areas to build the kind of long-term success that every artist, songwriter, and music industry employee needs. The investment that the record label makes is important, but the contribution of everyone associated with the artist, including the employees at the record label, managers, agents, album designers, and publicists, is equally important. Some artists and songwriters need a lot of guidance, and some of them have the ability to guide the rest of us, so we have to be extremely sensitive to the incredible diversity that exists within the creative community at large.

In this book, Mark Cabaniss helps you figure out where you fit in this great industry and understand the importance of music education, the essentials of songwriting, music copyright, revenue streams, performance, merchandising, and the basic truths that are essential for success. It is also very important to understand that the music industry does have many things in common with other industries. For example, the music industry needs accountants, lawyers, designers, publicists, executives, a skilled workforce, sales, marketing, and many other positions beyond the creative areas that are unique to the music industry. It is important to work hard, to maintain your focus, and most of all to realize that unlike in other industries, those working in the music industry must understand the ups and downs that occur because every record by every artist may perform very differently. Unlike industries where the end product is very definable, the music industry often has to understand that even records by the most successful artists and writers may vary in success (sales, chart action, critical response) from record to record and song to song. At the same time, while you're working in the music industry, you and your company will be subject to the same economic changes that affect our great country and the world at large.

In my own experience, my company has experienced times when we were at the very top, and we have experienced other times when we were not, but I have been told by many people that Curb Records may be the oldest record company that is still being operated by its original owner. Curb Records has created numerous jobs, started many artistic careers, and, most importantly, we have helped develop Curb colleges throughout the country and we have supported more than 100 charitable organizations. Without question, our success has been the result of the positive strengths of our artists, our employees, and our relationships with radio, film, television, and the new delivery systems that have evolved this century. It is hard to express the importance of the creative synergies that come from songwriters, producers, engineers, artists, and everyone involved in the creation of music. I have found that the most important thing is the need for long-term relationships inside and outside of the company. It is also important to understand as many genres of music as possible. Your career horizons will be greater if you can relate to pop music, rock music, R&B, country, gospel, and other music genres. When you start in the music industry, your chances of finding your first job will be greatly increased if you are prepared to work and learn in as many areas of the industry as possible. Mark's book helps you understand these areas, which is essential to putting the odds of success in your favor.

Mark has a unique perspective because he has worked in the industry, he has built his own entrepreneurial company, and he has been an educator devoted to our industry and its many changes throughout the years. The more that you learn about the music industry before you start, the greater your chances for success. On a personal note, I have always acknowledged that I was not great at anything; nevertheless, I have had some success in many areas of the industry that I never thought I could have. I was willing to try anything, and I learned that when you work with other people—in my case, often more talented than I am—it can lift a person to areas of opportunity that you might not be aware of. In my case, I was able to compose music commercials and motion picture songs and scores, perform as an artist, compose songs that won awards in pop and country genres, and become a *Billboard* producer of the year even though I didn't have the technical engineering abilities that so many others have. The most important thing is that I was open to trying everything, and I learned along the way that I could build a company by finding people who are more talented than I am in the numerous areas of the music industry. After 50 years in the industry, I am proud that our company is still competitive, and every day I am optimistic about our future and the ever-evolving new ways that young people are discovering to consume music.

Unlike other books, which are often long and complicated, Mark gives you a concise yet powerful understanding of the overall music industry and the individual opportunities that are unique to all of us. Regardless of each individual's music abilities, the more we understand the dynamics and the realities of the music business, the greater our chances to create a full life within the industry. Before you take your first steps in the music business, Mark's book and his experiences will give you a great head start and hopefully a pathway for a possible life in this amazing industry.

Mike Curb

ACKNOWLEDGMENTS

Note to the reader: Make sure you read all the names here . . . if you're not working with some of them now, you can only hope you will be someday.

First, my deepest thanks goes to the editor for this book, Natalie Mandziuk. Her input and ideas were invaluable and made this an infinitely better book than it would have been otherwise. Her encouragement and support, coupled with her unending kindness, professionalism, and patience with my hectic schedule, helped make it all possible. Also to the entire production and editorial team at Rowman & Littlefield, who did a fabulous job helping make this book what it is.

Next, to my mentors in the music business, my eternal appreciation for more than I can ever document here: Jim Van Hook, Buryl Red, Morty and Iris Manus, Billy Ray Hearn, and Don Hinshaw, all of whom helped shape my career.

To many of my dear friends in the music business who have helped and inspired me in so many ways, in particular Kathie Lee Gifford, David Pomeranz, Rupert Holmes, Andrew Surmani, Steven Raft, Ron Manus, Glenn Burtch, Lee Paynter, Kathy Fernandes, Tom Sabatino, Chris Titko, Bret Rhoades, Dwight Vicks, Eric Strouse, Jennifer Fry, Judy Henry, John Purifoy, Benjamin Harlan, Ruth Elaine Schram, Stan Pethel, Hal Hopson, Carl Gorodetsky, Dan Del Fiorentino, Elwyn Raymer, Alec Harris, John Shorney, Steve Shorney, and Stephen Bock.

To those teachers who helped shape my life and career choice: Helen Krause, William Thomas Jr., Dotty Dickson, Jean Mauney, Frances Welch, Larry Perry, Herbert Howard, and Jane Dunlap.

Special and heartfelt thanks to the legendary Mike Curb for his contribution to this book and his immeasurable and incredible contributions to the music business. Also to Doug Howard, Cheryl Slay Carr, and Rush Hicks for the opportunity and privilege to be a longtime member of the Belmont University family.

And finally, to Daniel Christian for his consistent encouragement throughout my writing of this book.

INTRODUCTION
Beginning the Journey

When I was knocking on doors long ago to get into the music business, among the many doors upon which I knocked was that of an industry veteran who evidently wanted to make sure I had the intestinal fortitude to enter such a treacherous and volatile industry. He said, "Are you *absolutely sure* you want to be in the music business, because it's very tough." I said without hesitation, "Yes. And *nothing* can stop me." After a pause, he said simply and confidently, "Then you'll make it."

That was almost 30 years ago, when the music business was booming. Nowadays, it's even tougher to make a living at it. For that reason, I've written this book for novices who desire to enter the music business or others who are considering a career change to get into it. I hope even seasoned professionals will find encouragement and useful information in this book . . . because in today's changing and more challenging than ever music business, a "road map" consisting of essential signposts and navigational tips is a good thing for everyone to help navigate the often-bumpy roads that are sometimes filled not only with potholes but also with landmines and booby traps.

There are those whom I consider professionals and nonprofessionals in the music business, and that's not based on how or if one gets paid for his or her work. I've known people who have worked in the music business for 30-plus years but, unfortunately, are very unprofessional. This book weaves in tips throughout to help the reader become a true music business *professional* . . . someone who does business in a manner that creates trust and with whom others want to work again and again.

The music business is about ups and downs and sideways and backward and all-the-way-around-wards. You can be an award winner one day

Fig I.1.   The Road to Success. *Illustration by Richard Duszczak*

and nowhere the next. It can be a champagne reception one month and a "hard candy Christmas" the next.

My late, great high school chorus teacher, Helen Krause, once said, "The only thing permanent in this world is change." How true. It has been said that those who are able to navigate change (and often reinvent themselves in the process) are the ones who will succeed most completely.

In the midst of the changing landscape of the music business, there are certain principles that remain constant. In my time in the industry, I've found that there are no real secret recipes to success, but there are essential *principles* and *techniques* (let alone solid, unchanging nuts-and-bolts information) upon which we can depend. These principles—when learned, internalized, and applied—can lead to a successful and wonderfully fulfilling career.

In addition to my work through the years as a music publisher, producer, and songwriter, I've taught music business as an adjunct faculty member at Belmont University in Nashville, Tennessee, for well over a decade. This book is a compilation of the nuts-and-bolts essentials that I've learned and taught to my students. I've included only the things that have resonated most with them, and they came back to me years afterward and said such essentials helped them in their life and career, for which I'm deeply grateful.

As cliché as it sounds, life is too short not to do something we enjoy. I have included several cartoons scattered throughout this book to add a touch of fun along your journey. Although the music business is serious business, it's also fun. If you enjoy what you do, then you're having fun. Every single day of my career in the music business hasn't always been enjoyable, but most of them have been. If you're making a living by doing something you enjoy, you'll never work a day in your life. I believe in the transforming power of music, and I agree with the late (and also great) Luciano Pavarotti when he said, "A life spent on music is a life beautifully spent." My hope is that this book will help you avoid any dead ends, unnecessary side trips, and wrong turns as you strategically chart your most effective path to success and fulfillment . . . while spending your life "beautifully."

There are a lot of books about the music business out there. In this one, I've attempted not only to give you the *essential* information to help put you on the fast track to true success but also to provide some "street wisdom" and motivational words that you won't necessarily find elsewhere.

So turn on your ignition, fasten your seat belt, grab the steering wheel, and hang on. Get ready for the ride of your life.

1

TO THINE OWN SELF BE TRUE

Why Do the Music Business?

As Polonius said in William Shakespeare's *Hamlet*: "To thine own self be true." Your chances of success in the music business (or any career for which you're suited) are greatly improved if you know yourself at the deepest level possible and are true to that self-knowledge. Then when the cold winds blow, good friends are hard to find, and your phone isn't ringing with offers, you are grounded and know what you're about . . . and nothing can shake you from your dreams. It's easy to be convicted about being in the tough music business when everything is going your way. It's harder when the chips are down. You'll have both moments, I promise, during your career. If you are secure in who you are and why you do what you do, you'll weather those inevitable storms. But it is up to you to get in touch with yourself at the deepest levels possible so you can make a living doing what you truly love.

First, the good news: As we saw in the introduction, opera singer Luciano Pavarotti said, "A life spent on music is a life beautifully spent." And if you are serious about spending your life in the music business—whether by making music yourself and/or helping other people make it and therefore reach more people by making it—that *is* truly a life beautifully spent. And not just because Mr. Pavarotti said it. It's because those of us who love music and have experienced its transforming power know that it has the ability to speak so deeply to us and change us in such wonderful, positive ways that we want others to experience its power and pleasure. It's a noble and worthy calling.

Now the bad news: Making a living in the music business is harder than it's ever been. Due to technology that has enabled millions to basically get music for free (otherwise known as stealing), the monetization of the music business is tough.

But don't let me discourage you. Seriously. I just want you to know what you're getting into.

1

That said, the music business is still one of the most exciting professions you can ever choose. According to the U.S. Department of Labor, Bureau of Labor Statistics, the average American spends more time working in a 24-hour period than any other single activity, including eating and sleeping.[1] How we spend our time working is how we will spend the better part of our lives.

One more statistic: A recent Gallup poll found that only 13 percent of employees throughout the world are truly engaged in their jobs.[2] Sobering facts!

CHART YOUR PATH

Author Richard Nelson Bolles, in his classic, perennially published book *What Color Is Your Parachute?*, lays out the tools for the reader to answer three vital questions in order to land the right job:

1. What are your best and most enjoyed skills?
2. Where do you want to use them?
3. Who at your desired place of employment can hire you?

These questions may seem obvious to some (and we'll spend more time on them later in the book), but I have known many people who never took the time to answer them authentically and ended up miserable in their job or career or at least employed at jobs in which they're bored and/or overqualified. If you haven't already answered the above questions authentically, then go buy Mr. Bolles's book and get started! (And/or visit his official website: www.jobhuntersbible.com.)

Let's assume, since you're reading this book, you're sure at this stage of your life that you want to pursue the music business (and *nothing* can stop you). You'll need to set goals on how to get where you're going (and if you're a seasoned professional in the music business and want to make a change to another segment of it, keep reading).

BEGIN WITH THE END IN MIND

Only when we truly know where we want to go can we get there.

Do you want to be a singer? A songwriter? A publisher? An agent? Producer? Engineer? An entertainment attorney? The list of functions in the music business is vast, with plenty of places for those people with different talents and abilities to fit in (which is good news). By being completely in touch with your "best and most enjoyed skills," you'll greatly increase your chances of success in the business.

Many people may know they want to be in the music industry but have no idea what they really want to do within it. At least they're being truthful when they say that and not giving an answer they think their professor, parents, or friends want to hear. When you have a foundation of self-truth and awareness, then you can get somewhere.

Therefore, if you're not sure where you fit in the vast expanse of the music business, keep reading. This chapter is also designed to help you become completely acquainted with those areas and functions so that you can make an informed decision.

Your career in the music business will most likely be an evolution. For example, you might begin as a singer and eventually become a producer or manager as the years go along due to a variety of circumstances in or out of your control. But it's highly unlikely your central core will change . . . in that what you enjoyed doing as a child, such as music, will remain. Those things you enjoyed as a child are excellent clues as to what you'll enjoy doing as an adult (and if you're fortunate, you'll be paid to do them).

That said, you need to have a clear starting point in your music business journey. You need to *focus*. Once you have a stated goal in mind, then you focus your efforts 100 percent toward accomplishing that goal. It may be a small, short-term goal ("I want to get a job in the music business anywhere doing anything . . . a receptionist, an assistant, a second engineer") or it may be a big goal ("I want to be a super successful, nationally known artist"), but whatever you goal is, it needs to be (1) written down, (2) measurable (have a date attached when you hope to accomplish it), and (3) challenging yet achievable.

Put your goal(s) on a small piece of paper (or save it in your phone) and put that paper in your wallet, your purse, or somewhere on your person! Have those goals with you every minute of your waking hours and dedicate yourself heart and soul to achieving those goals. These goals are *yours* . . . and no one else's. They should get you truly excited when you think about them. Visualize how it will feel once you accomplish those goals and the excitement and personal sense of achievement you'll have when you get there. And that's to say nothing of the benefit others will receive when you achieve your goals, because the best goals are those that benefit others and bring joy to their lives (and music is one of the best "joy-givers" around).

BE ON A MISSION

A ship can't successfully reach its destination without two key pieces of equipment: a steering wheel and a rudder. The steering wheel moves the rudder. The captain of the ship turns the wheel in order to make the rudder guide the ship.

A personal mission statement is akin to a rudder that guides your life. Having one is helpful in clarifying why you are on planet earth and what you hope to accomplish while you're here. It's different from a vision statement. A mission statement says "this is who I am and what I do," while a vision statement says "this is who I want to be in the future." Both have virtue, but for the purposes of this book, as a start, I encourage you to create a personal mission statement to get to the heart of who you are and what you're about. My mission statement is on my website (www.markcabaniss .com) in the "About" section. I hope you'll check it out as an example of how I shaped mine. If you do an Internet search on "mission statement," you'll find a wealth of resources on writing your own. And mission statements aren't "breakable." Change yours as much as you like until you get to the point you're satisfied with it. Start somewhere . . . even if it's a clumsy start . . . and write a simple statement describing who you are and what you want to do. That statement may evolve over the years, but most likely its core won't change.

Once the foundation is in place of knowing yourself at a deep level, you're ready to move on to the next step of exploring just what is in the music business universe that matches your best and most enjoyed skills.

THE MUSIC BUSINESS MACHINE:
WHERE DO YOU FIT IN?

Once you've determined your best and most enjoyed skills and that the music business is a good fit for those skills, you've got to get busy putting those skills to work somewhere. Will that be a large or small company? A public or privately held company? (Each has its pros and cons.) What about geographically? In what part of the world do you want to live? If you're starting out in the business, you might answer the above questions with "I'll work anywhere in the music business where I can get a job." And that's a good answer if you're starting, since once you're in the door, you can grow from there by showing you're outstanding. Ideally, you'll want to work somewhere that gives you a good career path, but something in the business is better than nothing when you're starting out (or changing careers). Therefore, it's to your advantage not to be too choosy if you want to pay the bills and start your career in the business.

The music business system is complex in many ways, but the overall concept of getting music to the consumer is relatively straightforward, although it has certainly radically changed over the years due to the Internet. But regardless of the changes, there are constants that have remained. And it takes a multitude of people to make it happen! The good news is that in that multitude, there is room for a variety of music lovers who want to make a living at it: people who are singers, players, producers, number crunchers, organizers, graphic designers, attorneys, merchandisers, retailers, managers, and on the list goes.

The music business is a bit like a gigantic machine that has a lot of different wheels in it that make it "go." In the classic movie *Willy Wonka and the Chocolate Factory*, the chocolate maker put ingredients in on one end of a device and out popped a piece of candy from the other. So the three basic components in that equation are ingredients + machine + consumer. Instead of chocolate ingredients, we put notes and music into the "music business machine" and out pops a song for consumption at the other end. Just as Willy Wonka knew the secrets of making great candy, so must we be keenly aware of the secrets to making great music and, equally important, how to get that great music out to the world.

The "music business machine" is the "device" that gets music out to the world. Machines have cogs and belts and wheels to keep them moving, and the music business machine has many moving parts to keep it going. Here are descriptions of the major elements in that machine so that you can start visualizing where and how you might fit in:

1. *Songwriter.* There's a popular bumper sticker on many Nashville cars that reads "It all begins with a song." Simple yet profound in the music business machine. If publishers don't have songwriters and songs, they must shut their doors. The art and craft of songwriting is among the most satisfying (and profitable) aspects of the music business. If you're disciplined, can work alone (or amicably with a cowriter . . . or several), and have a real talent for crafting music and/or lyrics, then this may be your calling. I say "real talent" because while raw talent can be honed and refined, it cannot be taught. Successful music publishers (if you can get songs in front of them . . . and with a lot of persistence, you can) will tell you honestly if you've got talent and if your songs are any good (if only in the form of acceptance or rejection of those songs). But don't let rejection get you down or set you back. My first published song was rejected several times before landing with a successful music publisher. It

went on to become one of their best-selling songs the year it was released (and is still selling more than 30 years after its initial release!). See chapter 13 in this book for a listing of numerous songwriting and other resources.

2. *Producer.* The producer is the "boss" of the recording. He or she hires all the musicians to be involved in recording and is sometimes even responsible for writing the material to be recorded (in addition to or instead of a songwriter . . . this depends on the producer's talents and defined role within the scope of the project that's being produced). Regardless of any possible writing, the producer is in charge of organizing the material and making it sound beautiful. He or she is the leader of the recording session and calls all the shots on what's played, when it's played, how it's played, the sounds that are used, or the vocals/instrumentals that are recorded and if the performers are singing/playing the correct notes desired by the composer, arranger, and/or orchestrator. The best producers are a positive, motivating force in a recording session, thereby gleaning the very best from the performers.

In addition to all of these aspects, producers must make sure the project stays on budget and is delivered on time to the record label. That's a pretty hefty job description! The producer can brainstorm on the spot in the studio and make changes to the existing musical material if he or she thinks it's just not working. However, if substantial changes are desired by the producer to the material's structure, words, melody, and so forth, it's best that the producer consult the material's writer(s) for permission, unless permission to make small (or large) changes was given prior to the recording session (although many times the writer is present since the writer is sometimes also the artist). The sum total of the producer's role requires that person to have fully functioning left- and right-brain capabilities—be creative, be organized—plus one final aspect: have great people skills. Working with artists, players, singers, engineers, and studio managers requires a producer to juggle a multitude of schedules and personalities . . . many of whom are creative types. Accordingly, the producer must be able to affably, efficiently, and effectively communicate to a wide variety of people his or her vision of the recording and get the most out of each of them in the most positive way (plus, the producer must have a nonflappable, "can-do" attitude if and when problems—technical or otherwise—arise).

And while the producer is the "boss" of the recording, the executive producer is the "ultimate boss" of the recording (though sometimes, depending upon the structure of the record label producing the recording, the executive producer of any given project may report to a record label president or vice president if the executive producer and label president/ VP aren't one and the same). The producer is accountable to the executive producer primarily to (1) deliver an excellent recording that meets or exceeds standards, (2) stay within the project budget, and (3) deliver the project on time.

3. *Artist/professional musician.* Of course, these are the people who make the magic happen! They're on the "front lines" of creating the actual sounds that we hear on the recordings, on television and film, in concerts, and so on. Artists are certainly professional musicians, but I delineate between the two here because artists are the ones who are at the forefront of the recording or tour, and professional musicians are the studio players, the working musicians who are playing the music. If you are a natural performer and have a true passion for communicating a message musically to an audience . . . either through recordings or live concerts . . . being an artist is for you. This is arguably the most personal job in the music business in that *you are the music* . . . you are making the music that is being heard, so if someone loves it (or doesn't), the artist feels that acceptance (or rejection) deeply. Accordingly, the reward (both creatively and financially) of being an artist is potentially the highest of any job in the music industry. A professional musician makes a living by playing or singing—be it on recordings, tours, the concert hall, the local bar and grill . . . you name it. These are the "behind the scenes" players whose names you rarely know, but the busiest of them all have performed on countless recordings. For example, the Nashville String Machine is a company that has contracted professional musicians for an endless number of recordings over the last 30 years. Everyone from Bruce Springsteen to Johnny Cash and Amy Grant to choral demonstration recordings have used players from this celebrated recording orchestra. It uses a contractor who hires the musicians for the respective gigs. Major and minor cities alike have local contractors who are looking to book professional musicians for various paying jobs. If you're a professional musician, it behooves you to make that contractor(s) aware of your talents (through a demo recording) so that you can get hired.

4. *Recording engineer.* For a producer on a recording session, aside from the artist(s), the recording engineer is the single most important person on a session. This person handles all the technical aspects of getting the music recorded properly: microphone choices, placement of musicians in the studio, how the musicians are recorded, track assignment, troubleshooting any technical problems as they may arise during the session, offering input on any creative questions the producer may have, and more. The best engineers not only execute these tasks but do so in an efficient, effective, and

genial manner. "Time is money," as is often said in a recording session, and that is 100 percent true. The best engineers (and producers) know how to balance the pressure of the clock and budget constraints against their own creative vision and desires for the project. A mix engineer (guided by the producer) executes the job of taking the multiple tracks that were recorded in a session and mixing/editing them together carefully and skillfully so as to create the most aesthetically pleasing sonic experience for the listener.

The mix engineer takes care of balancing and blending the multitude of sounds together after the recording is complete. Often the mix engineer and the recording engineer are one and the same. However, a producer may want to use different people in these roles simply because it's often good to have an objective, fresh "set of ears" to hear the project to mix it.

In addition to having a true passion for the technical side of the recording process, engineers should have excellent musical and creative instincts (an ability to read music is a wonderful plus), strong organizational skills, and the ability to tell great jokes when there's a technical glitch (while quickly fixing it!).

5. *Music publisher.* Simply put, the music publisher is a conduit to bridge the gap between the creator(s) of the music and the consumer. There are a variety of music publishers in the world: small, medium, and large . . . who publish every genre of music known to humanity! From pop to rock, classical to jazz, polka to hip-hop and rap . . . it's all there. If you're interested in working closely with songwriters as their sounding board (and sometimes as the shaper of their songs), an encourager, cajoler, challenger, friend, and fan, and have a sense of what will sell and what won't (at least to your chosen market), then the role of publisher could be for you. With its 50/50 mix of business and music, it's a perfect fit for someone with fully functioning left- and right-brain capabilities. (Music publishing is discussed more completely in chapter 6.)

6. *Business affairs.* This is the area in the music business that is concerned with legal issues: contracts—incoming and outgoing—and other ongoing legal issues that arise on a regular basis. For the sake of brevity, we'll throw accounting into this area as well. Depending upon the size of the company, a lot of contracts go in and out of a music publisher, record label, and so on. Even small companies have a lot of legal work that needs to be executed regularly. If you're looking for a job in this area in the music business, depending on the size of the firm with which you work, there may or may not be a full-time job available in the business affairs area. But there are law firms coast to coast that specialize in music business and/or entertainment

law (and other firms that simply have one person devoted to this area). And those companies that don't employ a person full time to handle legal (or accounting) duties need freelance people or legal/accounting firms to handle those tasks for them. Therefore, the opportunities for you if your talents/interests lie in the legal or accounting area are numerous. Attorneys also help out artists directly (see number 8 below for more details).

7. *Performing rights organizations (PROs)*. PROs are definitely a part of the business aspect of the music business (although the PROs are keenly aware of and involved in encouraging the creative process). The three U.S. PROs are ASCAP (American Society of Composers, Authors and Publishers), BMI (Broadcast Music, Inc.), and SESAC (which stands only for SESAC nowadays, but it originally stood for the Society of European Stage Authors and Composers). In short, these organizations track public performances of copyrighted music, collect money from the public music users, and then pay the owners and writers of that music for those public performances. Chapter 8 covers PROs in more detail.

8. *Artist management.* If you're not longing for the spotlight but want to help facilitate the career of someone who is, then artist management is an area you should investigate. Included in this category are personal manager, business manager, publicist, and attorney.

A personal manager is the single most important member of an artist's team. This person guides an artist in all areas as he or she generally functions not only directly in providing input on business, marketing, and creative decisions but also helps assemble an artist's team and interacts with that team on a regular basis. A business manager, in short, handles the money for an artist (expenses, taxes, etc.). A publicist generates and manages publicity for an artist, which includes coordinating press relationships, interviews, and so forth. An attorney does what attorneys do regarding legal matters but in this context advises an artist on contracts. The best attorneys who work directly with artists also have a hand in helping shape the artist's complete business life (in conjunction with the personal manager).

9. *Live performance.* Since the record business had been in transition for several years (with physical record sales declining while digital record sales have not replaced the decline as robustly as record companies and artists hoped), live performances have become all the more important as revenue streams. Employment opportunities in this area include concert production and promotion, arts administration (symphony orchestras, classical artist management, etc.), ticketing, and public relations. If you enjoy working with the public and being on the "front lines" of bringing live performances to the world, this area of the business could be perfect for you.

10. *Retail.* As noted earlier, the manner in which music is delivered to the consumer nowadays has changed and evolved, and retail is one of the main "wheels" in the music business machine that has been affected (meaning traditional brick-and-mortar establishments). Although there are still some record-only independent brick-and-mortar stores that exist today, most of them have gone away. When you find records these days at the retail level, you'll find them at "big box" retailers (Best Buy, Target, Walmart, etc.). There are some other (unexpected) locations where you'll find physical CDs, such as gift stores, drug stores, restaurants, and other boutique and specialty shops, but those locations for records are few and far between. Internet retailers (such as Amazon) have become the largest retailers of music. And the largest music retailer of them all is iTunes. If

In the Mix: Do You Love Music?

As I tell my students, "We're not selling concrete in the music business." Not that there's anything wrong with selling concrete. Or insurance. Or real estate. Those things are great in and of themselves, I'm sure, but when you're in the music business, you're ultimately selling emotions. And that can be a tricky thing. That's not to say you have to be hyperemotional to be in the music business. You don't necessarily need to read music to be in the music business. And you don't need to be directly involved in the making of music (if you're in the royalty or accounting side of it, for example). But if you choose to make a living one way or another in the music business, you need to love music or, in other words, have an emotional attachment to it. Period. For example, you need to have songs in your past that had a lasting impact on you. You need to enjoy listening to music as one of your favorite things to do. And if you also perform it publicly and/or privately, all the better. Having a genuine emotional connection with music and believing in its transforming power will help fuel your fire to get out of bed every day to make a living at it. Otherwise, go sell concrete. Because if you don't have a passion for music, then you won't have the staying power to stick with it through all the inevitable ups and downs the business brings (let alone understand those creative types who are emotional and passionate about it). Love music and chances are it will love you back. I call my house "the house that music built." And I can "feel the love" every time I step into it at the end of a long day.

you're a lover of retail stores, working with the public, and aspects of merchandising, pricing, displaying, and so on (all of which are also factors with Internet retailers), then music retail could be a great fit for you.

The above list is by no means exhaustive, but it does contain the primary components of the music business machine . . . any of which are worthy full-time employment opportunities.

NOTES

1. U.S. Department of Labor, Bureau of Labor Statistics, American Time Use Survey, https://www.bls.gov/tus/.

2. Gallup, *State of the American Workplace: Employee Engagement Insights for U.S. Business Leaders* (Washington, DC: Gallup, Inc., 2013).

2

IT ALL BEGINS WITH A SONG

You can't make a living in most businesses if you don't have something to sell. And in the music business, we sell . . . *music!* And if we don't have music, we have nothing to sell. And what we have won't sell if it's not good.

There's a lot of music in the world. Naturally, some of it is good, some of it is bad, and some of it is in-between. As with any art form, beauty is in the eye of the beholder. This chapter isn't concerned with determining which music is "good" or "bad" per se but rather with agreed-upon basic foundations that help give music artistic and commercial appeal. One certainly cannot discount the tremendous impact a great performance of a song has on the appeal of that song, but even the best performance in the world can't camouflage a badly written song. And regardless of whether or not you are going to be strictly on the creative side or the business side of the music business (and you'll possibly have one foot in both worlds . . . especially if you have fully functioning left and rights sides of your brain!), it behooves you to know what constitutes a great song.

Volumes of books have been written on songwriting, and this chapter is no attempt to thoroughly cover the vast subject of songwriting. However, this chapter does present the basics of songwriting . . . those elements of solid song construction anyone in the music business should know in order to appreciate great songs and judge untried songs if in the role of deciding a song's potential success. Songwriters and publishers obviously need to know the ingredients of a hit song, but so do A&R (artists and repertoire) people, artists, managers . . . anyone who has a role in the music business. For example, if you're an artist manager or attorney, how can you decide if you want to represent a particular songwriter if you don't know if the songs that person is writing are marketable and have potential earning

13

power? If you know the basic elements of great songs, you can make an informed decision on whether to move forward or not.

Astounding as it may seem, there are music business executives (past and present) who were/are heads of record and publishing companies but were/are woefully inadequate when it comes to understanding the *basic elements* of a great song. And eventually it caught up (or will catch up) with them (e.g., with shrinking sales and market irrelevance). How can someone who is hiring people for their team (who make decisions about what to publish and record) know whom to hire if they can't at least understand the basics of solid song construction?

Warning: As with any creative endeavor, there's always the mysterious "wow" factor . . . *wow* meaning that indescribable element present in a song that you can't quite put your finger on and that makes the song outstanding. So the warning here is that although we will explore elements of great songs in this chapter, just following the "recipe" of those ingredients to a T doesn't necessarily mean you'll write hit songs every time (of course).

Songwriting is very similar to the art of cooking in that you must write . . . and then listen to the song being performed . . . write and listen again . . . and again (and again!) to learn what does and doesn't work. Songwriters should study the craft of songwriting through the myriad of resources available to them (books, seminars, videos, songwriting clubs, etc.). They should also should seek out unbiased people who are their target audience to "consume" their music and then listen to those consumers to learn what they really think. As the old saying goes, the proof of the pudding is in the eating!

Anyone can follow the recipe to bake a cake, but it takes that (sometimes elusive) wow factor to be a great chef who creates unforgettable meals. Some people spend the better part of their lives learning how to be a great chef . . . through trial and experimentation, study, and so on. And the people who eat that food give the chef the most useful information about whether or not the chef's cooking is any good (and that means learning from those consumers who aren't necessarily relatives or loved ones and who will most likely be honest about whether they like the food).

THE TOP 10 INGREDIENTS OF A GREAT SONG

1. Fresh Concept

This is the basic ingredient for any great song. Does the world need another song about romance? Well, yes, if it's somehow an original take on the subject (or frames it uniquely). For example, consider "Shape of You," a pop song written by Ed Sheeran with Steve Mac and Johnny McDaid, with additional writing credits given to Kandi Burruss, Tameka "Tiny" Cottle, and Kevin "She'kspere" Briggs as Sheeran interpolated the TLC's song "No Scrubs" into "Shape of You." This song hit number one on the music charts of 44 countries, including *Billboard*'s Hot 100 chart. It also became the best-performing song of 2017 and won a 2017 Grammy Award. If that weren't enough, it became the most-streamed song to date on Spotify with more than 1.32 billion streams![1] Obviously, the song struck a *big* chord (no pun intended) with romantics around the world because it tapped into universal emotions in a fresh way. It clearly had the wow factor.

I often use what is called the "Guiding Star" for each song I write. The Guiding Star is the ultimate message of the song. I write this down as it emerges after I have solidified the song concept and then keep it at the top of the lyric page as I write lyrics, always keeping that Guiding Star in mind so that everything in the lyric helps support and communicate that message/concept.

2. Appropriate Title

The right title for a song often helps it practically write itself. The title should be a connect, not a disconnect (meaning the title should tell the listener basically what to expect from the song). A title can also set the mood of the song, but of course it can't convey every aspect of a song in advance (nor should it). But it should help telegraph what the song is about and pique the listener's interest as to what he or she might expect and/or cause the listener to think, "Hmmm . . . that sounds interesting. Tell me more." Titles such as "Shake It Off" (Taylor Swift/Max Martin/Shellback), "Purple Rain" (Prince), "Lyin' Eyes" (Don Henley/Glenn Frey), or "Goodbye Yellow Brick Road" (Elton John/Bernie Taupin) set the stage for unforgettable, lasting hit songs.

3. Solid Structure

In its most basic form, music is *contrast and repetition*. You need to give the listener something to hang on to in order to best digest the message you're imparting. Popular music has several forms that are commonly used. Some of the most common song forms are A-A-B-A (ternary), which contains verse-verse-chorus-verse. Examples: "Over the Rainbow" and

"Yesterday." Another popular form is A-B-A-B (binary), which contains verse-chorus-verse-chorus. Examples: "Material Girl" or "Sunrise, Sunset" (from the musical *Fiddler on the Roof*).

There's also strophic form (AAA), but this is used more with hymns, not popular songs. Songwriting tutorials and in-depth form analysis abound on the Internet with a simple search.

4. Compelling Introduction

Every part of a song matters, but the introduction is one of the most important parts. An introduction sets the mood to your song. It's like the first scene of a play . . . it portends what is to come. Make your song's introduction appropriate for what is to come. Perhaps it is a snippet of your primary melodic theme (or a slight variation on that theme), so when that theme does appear later with lyrics, it already feels familiar to the listener. There are several types of unique hit song introductions where singers hummed (Barbra Streisand—"The Way We Were"), whistled (Billy Joel—"The Stranger"), or just sang "la, la, la, la!" (the Carpenters—"Sing"). Sometimes, in rare cases, there is no song introduction at all in an effort to create an immediacy (akin to the curtain going up on a musical without an overture). For example, "Good Vibrations" (recorded by the Beach Boys) begins without an introduction. Such an approach can work very effectively.

5. Well-Constructed Lyrics

First and foremost, a song's words must come from an authentic place in the writer's personal experience. For example, if you want to write about a broken heart, you'd better have had one before. The rhymes should feel natural, and the language should be simple, believable, and relatable. The opening words should cause the listener to want to keep listening and pay attention. Examples of classic hit pop songs that begin with memorable opening lines abound . . . take a look at any of your favorites and analyze why and how they caught and kept your attention.

Other important considerations in lyric writing:

- *Phrasing structure and length.* What form listed above (or another) best helps convey the message (Guiding Star) you're attempting to communicate? How long will your phrases be? Many beginning songwriters fall into the trap of writing phrases that are too long and hard to perform, let alone sink in for the listener.

- *Rhyming.* How will you arrange the rhymes? Should they be perfect rhymes (such as *how/now*) versus false, imperfect rhymes (such as *life/despite*).
- *Closure.* Equally important to how you begin a song lyrically is how you end it. This is the final thought that will hopefully linger in the listener's mind, along with the power of the entire experience.

6. Melody

The melody is what gives wings to the lyrics. It should be a connect and not a disconnect, meaning the music is there to serve the words. For example, if the lyric in your song is about reaching higher and higher, the obvious approach is for the melody to go higher and higher (but still within singing range of the artist!). Other considerations include not lingering too long on high or low notes so as to make the song comfortably singable not only by a professional artist but by those who want to sing along in their car (the vast majority of the people who will sing your song and buy it). Avoid illogical leaps in the melody as well, which also lead to uncomfortable singing. However, a melody should have certain unexpected movement and changes so as to keep it unpredictable. It's a balancing act between singable yet fresh and surprising. Other considerations are the moments of silence that are built into a melody, which can be as important as the notes. Sometimes what is unsaid has as much of an impact as what is said. For example, in the Whitney Houston version of the Dolly Parton–written song "I Will Always Love You," Houston takes a dramatic pause before launching into her final, heart-wrenching rendition of the chorus. It's a very powerful use of a brief moment of silence.

7. Harmony/Progressions

This is what gives life and richness to the melody. *Harmony* is the foundational grounding to the melody. If you're not careful, your harmony can make your melody (and song) sound dated. That's bad, of course, unless you're striving for a retro sound. But the best harmony is akin to a great melody that supports its lyric: The harmony supports and complements the melody. A *progression* is the series of chords (harmonies) that recur throughout a song. The chords you choose may go upward or downward or skip back and forth. Beginning songwriters (and veterans alike) are well advised to study successful songs (especially your favorite ones) and analyze the chords and progressions to see what worked. Of course, you shouldn't duplicate those songs, but you can glean ideas and learn new chords and progressions that can inspire you to reach new and fresh heights in your own writing.

8. *Length*

How long a song lasts is always a consideration, depending on where and how the song is used. If the song is going to be played on the radio, it should last (typically) anywhere from three and a half to four minutes. Songs can certainly be shorter or longer, but this is the standard range of length. If the song is in a theatrical work, it can certainly be longer if need be.

9. *Beat/Rhythm*

The beat and rhythm are what drive a song and help the listener connect with the song at its most "base" level. All the above elements of the song can evoke both emotional and cerebral responses, but the beat/rhythm (or tempo/speed) somehow seem to manifest themselves physically in the listener to whom the music of the song appeals. A great beat—be it fast and percussive or slow and seductive—stirs our emotions. Make sure the rhythms and beat you set up for your song support everything about it: words, melody, harmony, and so forth.

10. *Great Ending*

All elements of a song must work together cohesively to create an enjoyable (and hopefully memorable) experience for the listener, and the ending is the final consideration in creating a great song. Although it should be consistent with what has come before it, there's nothing to say you can't have an ending that is surprising or unexpected if that ultimately helps make your song more entertaining and memorable. There are several classic hits with memorable, unexpected twists at the end: "A Boy Named Sue," recorded by Johnny Cash; "Cat's in the Cradle," recorded by Harry Chapin; and "Escape (the Pina Colada Song)," recorded (and written) by Rupert Holmes. For inspiration and instruction, check out any of these songs or others with surprise endings to learn how their songwriters ended them memorably.

After you've put all of these building blocks into place, if you're not excited about the song, then chances are no one else will be either. Ask yourself,

"Does the song truly inspire me?" While you were writing it, you should have had those fun "aha!" moments that made you think, "Now *this* really sounds great! I can't wait to share this with the world!" If not, then you need to rewrite it . . . or at least the parts of it that don't excite you. Besides, songs aren't really written anyway . . . they're rewritten and rewritten until you know in your heart and with your musical sensitivities that each is finished. Remember, songs aren't "breakable" . . . meaning when you change something, you can always go back and restore the original thought (as long as you have a system for accurately preserving what you did before, which is much easier these days with computers). And if, after letting the song "breathe" for a day or two and not looking at it, you return to the song and find it doesn't do anything for you, it's probably time to put it in "the trunk." You might be driving down the road a year later when something hits you out of the blue that helps unlock the mystery of what didn't excite you about that particular song, and suddenly you're on fire to make those change(s) and *voilá*, you've created something about which you're excited and proud.

Sometimes writers paint themselves into a corner with a title, a concept, or music/lyrics that ultimately don't pan out or excite them. Don't worry! Cut your losses and move on to another song about which you can get excited before you spend any more time on a song that doesn't inspire or excite you.

Another fun aspect of writing a song is "casting" the song . . . that is, who is the artist you dream of recording it? Of course, if you're a beginning songwriter, having anyone record your song is exciting. But as you write the song, it's not a bad idea to have a performer in mind who might bring it to life. Accordingly, if you envision your song being sung by Beyoncé, you should write it in her vocal range. But it's probably a long shot that she'll ever record your song (though don't let that dream die!), so if your cousin ends up recording it and it's out of her range, that's an easy fix.

PITCHING YOUR SONG

Let's assume you've finished your latest song and followed the above principles of solid songwriting. Bravo! Now it's time to get down to business and get the song to land on desk of someone who has the power to get it out there. Of course, the first stop to accomplishing that task is a music publisher.

There's much more regarding the mechanics of music publishing later in this book, but for the purposes of this chapter, finding not only *a* publisher but *the* publisher for your song is (apart from creating the song) the single most important decision you can make on behalf of your song "baby." Here, therefore, are top tips for placing your baby (uh, song) with a music publisher. They're not only tips but tried-and-true principles that I'm calling "commandments."

THE 10 COMMANDMENTS OF
GETTING YOUR SONG PUBLISHED

1. Make a Good Demo

First, you'll need a demo (demonstration) recording of the song. Don't go out and spend a lot of money on making a demo. If you yourself don't have a decent singing voice, find a friend who does. Publishers understand that songwriting demos aren't necessarily sung by the best voices. Any publisher worth his or her salt can see through (or "hear through," as it were) a less-than-perfect vocal performance on a demo. Of course, you don't want your demo to sound so bad that it doesn't present your song in the best light. It's just that you don't need to spend hundreds and hundreds of dollars on a demo. If you can find a reasonably priced local recording studio, great . . . use it. Most of the studio business has shifted to home studios these days, so if you don't have your own home studio, use whatever connections you have to uncover one and then negotiate a reasonable price to use it (if it's a friend's studio, maybe you can barter . . . treat him or her to lunch in exchange for an hour or two in the studio!). And if you can't find a good studio to record your demo, consider a local church or school. These places usually have a decent piano (make sure it's in tune) and an acoustically acceptable room in which to record.

2. Make a Lead Sheet

A lead sheet consists of the song's lyrics, notated melody, and chord symbols. Most songwriters are capable of making a lead sheet, but some aren't (the great Irving Berlin, composer of "God Bless America," "White Christmas," and a host of other standards, never learned to read or write music). If you can't make your own lead sheet, there are those who will notate one for a reasonable price. And it's entirely acceptable to present your song with only a lyric sheet (no notes or chord symbols). A lead sheet is optimum, but lyric sheets will also do. Of course, in the case of a more involved work (choral, orchestral, classical, etc.), notated music is a must for submission.

3. Don't Shoot in the Dark

Akin to magazine publishers, music publishers have a specific niche, genre, or segment of the market they serve. Do your homework before you send a piece for publication consideration. If the publisher has a website (most do), visit their website to learn all about that publisher. Are they publishing the sort of music you're writing? If you are the somewhat rare songwriter who can write authentically in diverse styles, that certainly increases your chances of getting your songs published. Do the publishers you're considering already have the sort of song you've written? Do they take unsolicited submissions? Most publishers who take unsolicited submissions have a section on their website devoted to listing the criteria for what, when, and how they'll accept such submissions.

4. Write a Cover Letter

A simple, brief cover letter explaining a bit about the song and how it came to be, along with a quick bit of background about yourself, is a good introduction to the submission.

5. Include an SASE

If you want your material returned (if the publisher rejects it), it's best to include a self-addressed, stamped envelope along with your submission. If music publishers paid postage for returning all the material they reject each year, they would spend thousands of dollars annually. Plus, if they return your material, you can simply pack it up for the next publisher to whom you're sending it.

6. Submit Singularly

Don't send your music to more than one publisher at a time. Although it sounds like a dream come true to have your song desired by more than one publisher, it's not. If you have to go back to a publisher to whom you submitted a song and tell them you've decided to sign the song to their competitor (to whom you simultaneously sent the song for consideration), that publisher isn't going to be pleased (and you've possibly burned a bridge with the publisher who didn't get your song). It's a maddening feeling to have to wait (and sometimes wait) for a publisher to send you a decision before submitting it elsewhere, but it's worth it as you attempt to build strong relationships with as many publishers as possible.

7. Don't Send Too Much

Music publishers are often inundated with unsolicited submissions in addition to everything they do each day to keep the doors open. Pick your two (maximum three) best pieces to submit . . . but no more. If you develop a relationship with a publisher (based on publishing something of yours to begin with), you can eventually increase how many things you send at once (with their permission, of course).

8. Have a Connection

If possible, network your way into knowing someone—practically anyone—at the publisher with whom you want to submit your song(s). If you are able to get your foot in the door with that publisher one way or another with someone, then that person will probably know the decision-maker to whom you need to submit your material. Get an email address if possible, that way you're not calling a busy editor out of the blue to ask about submission timetables, guidelines, and so on. Email the person a brief, cordial note inquiring if they take unsolicited submissions, if so what are they currently looking for, and so forth. If you've done your homework as noted above in point 3, you'll be all the more equipped to communicate intelligently to the publisher as to their style, timetable, and other items. By making some sort of personal, initial connection with the decision-maker, you stand a better chance that your song will get reviewed sooner.

9. Timing Is Everything

Sometimes even if your song is great, it may hit the right publisher (one that publishes the type of music you're writing) at the wrong time. Perhaps that particular publisher recently received a song very similar to yours, so they don't need another one just like it. Or they already have a song akin to the one you sent them in their catalog. Publishers don't always have time to explain such things if they reject your song for that reason, so don't automatically take their rejection as meaning your song isn't good enough. However, if your song is rejected by a number of publishers, you should possibly rethink it or put it away and move on to the next song(s) you want to pitch. (There are no failures in life . . . only learning experiences. Let each song rejection you receive be a learning experience.)

10. Be Patient

In addition to reviewing new material for possible publication, music publishers are engaged in a myriad of duties and challenges each and every day. So allow anywhere from 9 to 12 weeks before expecting to receive a publication decision.

DO YOU NEED A COLLABORATOR?

Rodgers and Hammerstein, John and Taupin, Lerner and Loewe, Weil and Mann, Alan and Marilyn Bergman, the Sherman Brothers . . . and the list could go on of world-famous songwriting duos that enjoyed (and enjoy) smooth sailing. And there are stories of partnerships that were often strained and rancorous (e.g., Gilbert and Sullivan). But there is no denying that two heads are sometimes better than one.

Collaboration in songwriting can be a wonderfully productive and rewarding experience. Or it can be a nightmare. It depends on the person with whom you're collaborating, of course. There are many things to take into consideration. First and foremost, if you're not completely comfortable and confident/competent in writing either the words or the music, you'll need to find a collaborator who does what you can't do. Next, you'll need to find someone with whom you "click" creatively (not necessarily personally, although that doesn't hurt). Some of the most commercially successful songwriting partnerships were between people who had very little in common other than their ability to write together and turn out hit songs. So be it! You're not getting married, after all. But the songs you create together are, in essence, your babies and will link you together for the life of the song (which you hope is a long time), so if you're going to have a collaborator for some or all of your creative work, choose carefully. So how do you choose a collaborator carefully?

Is your potential collaborator's work ethic similar to your own? Is he or she willing to spend the time necessary to really make the song great (e.g., is that person going to pull his or her weight when it comes to the workload)? Does he or she work at hours similar to your own? And how is this person about money? Can you trust this person to reimburse you for his or her share of the cost of the demo if you write a check for it? And does he or she have a reasonably sized ego that won't demand constant attention, stroking, and so on?

Plus, there are financial considerations. You will obviously receive less royalty money when you bring on a collaborator. Generally, the royalty split between a lyricist and composer is 50/50, but that's negotiable depending on how things actually play out during the creation of the song. Perhaps the composer came up with the title of the song and wrote half of the lyrics. In that case, the fair thing might be a 70/30 split. But again, that depends on how flexible each party is in the relationship. These things should be discussed up front (otherwise, you might end up as Gilbert and Sullivan and other disappointed collaborators who wound up suing each other in a rancorous legal battle).

If you're fortunate enough to work with a superstar singer who isn't a songwriter, those superstars will sometimes insist on being credited as one of the songwriters (and on receiving a portion of the royalties accordingly, even if he or she hasn't lifted a finger to help, other than possibly sharing a few ideas here and there). If the singer's recording of your song will guarantee massive exposure (and songwriting royalties), the best advice here is "do it!" Plus, this can lead to other songwriting gigs with other high-profile artists and writers.

At the end of the day, the construction of great music is worth all the work, blood, sweat, and tears . . . especially when you're in a restaurant or concert hall . . . or wherever . . . and hear *your* song performed and that song inspires, cajoles . . . or otherwise moves the listener as you hoped it would when you wrote it. There's nothing else like it in the world, and

In the Mix: Music, Money, and Magistrates

Novice songwriters are often (naturally) confused about the best way to be remunerated for their songwriting. There are a lot of sharks out there waiting to take your money and promise you fame and fortune. And many times, the budding songwriter is left with nothing but broken promises and empty pockets. As stated elsewhere in this book, *never* pay to have your song published. Publishers pay *you* to publish your song. Therefore, what should you expect to be paid for your song, and how does that whole process work?

First, if your song is a great song (and of course you think that, or at least you should), it will be attractive to any number of publishers. That publisher will want to sign the song (i.e., offer you a contract for the song)

in which they will pay you a royalty. Royalty rates vary depending on how the song will be used (e.g., recordings, film, television, print, stage). Publishing revenue streams are discussed at length in chapter 6, but for the purposes of this discussion, you should know that generally a royalty is the best route to go (vs. work for hire, which is also defined in chapter 6, along with the pros and cons of a royalty vs. work for hire). As for the actual amount you can expect for your song if you choose the work-for-hire route, naturally the higher, the better! Everything is relative, and the amount that is paid for a song varies based on the type of use. You shouldn't "shop" your song around for the highest rate since you don't want to be caught in the pickle of having your song accepted by a publisher, only to have another publisher accept it soon thereafter, and leaving you to inform the second publisher that the song is already signed with another publisher. Submit your song to only one publisher at a time, and don't submit it to another until you've heard from the one with whom the song is currently under consideration.

Beginning songwriters sometimes engage the services of an attorney to negotiate their deals for them. If you use an attorney who isn't familiar with the music business, he or she sometimes naively asks for more than is given in standard publishing deals . . . for example, that the songwriter should retain part or full ownership of the song. In a case such as that, the publisher becomes merely an administrator of the copyright, and publishers are in the publishing business (i.e., they own copyrights). Therefore, there's little or no incentive for publishers to sign the song in such a scenario. Beginning songwriters should seek reputable, successful publishers to sign (publish) their songs. Hit songwriters with an established track record of years of success can entertain the notion of retaining some (or all) ownership of their songs. But in the beginning, it's best for songwriters to sign over all the "bundle of rights" to their song to the publisher (the bundle of rights are defined in chapter 3).

But how to know if a publisher is reputable and successful? Through your network, try to find someone who has had a song published with that publisher and ask that person questions such as "Did they treat you with respect and not make any surprising changes to your song without your permission?" "Were you credited correctly for your contribution to the song (wherever the song appeared . . . such as recordings)?" "How often do they pay royalties and were you paid on time?" And of course, "Did they promote your song to get it the sort of exposure (and revenue) that is satisfactory to you?" Often publishers will list names (and even bios) of their prominent songwriters, which is another way you can identify and approach a few of them to learn of their experiences with said publisher.

the world (or at least a small corner of it) can benefit from your unique idea called a . . . *song*.

NOTE

1. "Shape of You," Wikipedia, https://en.wikipedia.org/wiki/Shape_of_You.

3

THE BIG FOUNDATION
Music Copyright

Envision a world . . . without music!

Not a pretty sight. That's not going to happen, of course. But without the copyright law, there is no music *business*. There will certainly always be music, but without a copyright law there would be *much* less of it in terms of availability and the creation of quality new works. There would be no financial incentive to create music and therefore no means to make a living at it. Songwriters, music publishers, artists, record companies, agents, tour managers . . . everyone . . . would be out of a job instantly . . . to say nothing of all other creative endeavors that rely on the protection of intellectual property to make a living. The copyright law protects a lot more than just music. Everything from other artistic works (paintings, drawings, photographs, sculptures, etc.) to dramatic works (plays, choreography, screenplays, etc.) to sound recordings and television broadcasts are protected by the copyright law.

Therefore, everyone in the creative business must constantly be vigilant to guard and protect copyright. The very livelihoods of everyone in the music business depend on copyright's healthy existence.

Today's U.S. copyright law is really not that old in the grand scheme of things, leaving it somewhat open to challenge. And with today's ever-changing music business world and mechanisms of content delivery (constantly influenced by the Internet, it seems), there's always someone out there—large and small companies, organizations, or other special interest groups—who are desirous of obliterating copyright (believe it or not). Because if people don't have to pay for music, then their businesses (which use music in a large or small way) can thrive all the more, right? Of course right. They want the piper to play but don't want to pay the piper.

It behooves us to understand a bit of copyright law's beginnings and how we got to where we are today, let alone how it works. The current copyright law had a long road to get to where it is currently, reaching all the way back to the 15th century (at a time when the Pied Piper was mythically making music).

COPYRIGHT BEGINNINGS

One could say that copyright has its earliest beginnings with the invention of movable type by Johannes Gutenberg in the 15th century. Gutenberg invented the world's first printing press that had moveable type. This led to a printing revolution in Europe, which played a pivotal role in publishing and making books available to the masses. Before Gutenberg's invention, books were copied by hand(!). Hard to believe, but that's the way thing were in the 15th century regarding publishing. There were probably plagiarists back then, but prior to the invention of movable type, it was much more difficult to rip someone off. With the advent of the eventual widespread distribution of original ideas, anyone with a printing press could duplicate others' ideas and work at will—and profit from them. Poems, maps, books, pamphlets, music . . . you name it . . . became easy "pickins" for anyone to reproduce for a profit. This created the need for a reasonable control of such dissemination of ideas, but it began as a means to control what people were saying about those in power.

It was King Charles II—along with Parliament—who enacted the Licensing of the Press Act 1662. This act of the Parliament of England was intended to prevent abuses in publishing of printing unlicensed and potentially treasonous materials. Printing presses couldn't even be set up without notification to an agency named the Stationers' Company. If this law was broken, severe penalties resulting in fines and even imprisonment were levied against offenders.[1] As a result of this act, the term *royalty* was born as a means to describe remuneration for licensed printing and publishing. When the House of Commons did not renew the Licensing Act in 1695, unauthorized and rampant printing and publishing started all over again. Legitimate publishers who had rightfully reaped the benefits of the Licensing Act urged Parliament to respond, and respond it did, with the Statute of Anne (Copyright Act 1710). The statute is recognized as the first copyright law in the world since it was the first law that protected the rights of the creators. Under this statute, creators' works were protected for 14 years, with a possible renewal term of an additional 14 years. Copyright was up and running!

EARLY COPYRIGHT LAW
IN THE UNITED STATES

The First Congress implemented the copyright provision of the U.S. Constitution in 1790. The Copyright Act of 1790 was modeled on the Statute of Anne. This provision granted American authors the right to print, reprint, or publish their work exclusively for a period of 14 years. The copyright could then be renewed for another 14. This law, as in subsequent copyright laws, was intended to provide incentive to authors, artists, and scientists to create original works by providing creators with a "limited duration monopoly."[2] Therefore, the most succinct definition of copyright is a "limited duration monopoly."

As the 20th century dawned, technology kept moving faster and faster, challenging copyright laws to keep up. New devices using music, such as the player piano, were invented, requiring modifications to be made to the copyright law. In 1905, President Theodore Roosevelt championed a new copyright law, and after several years of development and debate, the Copyright Act of 1909 was born.

THE CURRENT COPYRIGHT LAW

As referenced earlier, "The only thing permanent in this world is change," esteemed music educator Helen Krause once said. Change continued to come at a barreling pace in the 20th century, causing the 1909 Copyright Act to again be overhauled. Between 1909 and the 1970s, new devices and technologies flourished: motion pictures, radio, television, records, cassettes, photocopiers, satellites, and even computers. After two decades of research and debate, congress passed the Copyright Act of 1976 (which came into effect on January 1, 1978).

While advances in the aforementioned flourishing technologies certainly provided incentive to advance the existing copyright law, the United States' anticipated participation in the Berne Convention was clearly a factor. The Berne Convention codified several aspects of the modern copyright law (most notably that a copyright is legal when it's in a so-called fixed form—that is, on a lead sheet or tangible recording—rather than requiring official registration with the copyright office).[3]

So how long does a copyright last with the passing of the Copyright Act of 1976? (There was a subsequent Copyright Term Extension Act passed in 1998.) Here's the scoop:

1. "For works published between 1923 and 1963, there's an initial 28-year term but then must be renewed for an additional 67 years (for a total protection of 95 years)."
2. "For works published between 1964 and 1977, they are protected for 28 years plus an *automatic* 67-year second term for a total of 95 years of protection."
3. "For works published after 1977 the term of copyright is life of the author plus 70 years. In the case where the work has more than one author, protection is 70 years after the death of the last surviving author."[4]

Works published before 1923 fall into the public domain (which means they are no longer protected by copyright). And why would music ever become a part of the public domain?

The thinking on the part of the lawmakers is that if a copyright has lasted 70 years after the death of the last surviving author, it has sufficiently provided remuneration not only for the original author(s) but for his or her heirs. And if a work has lasted that long, it has become part of the fabric of the culture and should therefore belong to "the public" at large.

A common question (especially from beginning songwriters) is, "Should I have my song copyrighted?"

According to the copyright law, once a work is in a "fixed, tangible form" it is *legally copyrighted*.[5] Therefore, it need not be registered with the U.S. Copyright Office to be legally copyrighted. (However, it should be *registered* to assure proof of ownership especially should ownership of said copyright ever be challenged. More on registration later.)

That said, my personal philosophy is that songwriters needn't register their songs with the U.S. Copyright Office . . . since their songs are legally copyrighted when in a "fixed, tangible form" (e.g., notated on a lead sheet, sung on a demo placed on a CD, even scribbled on the back of an envelope!). One's goal should be to get the song published by a reputable music publisher who will then register the song (and pay the registration fee) for the songwriter. Until the song is published, guard it carefully and share it only with those you trust not to steal it from you! Stealing certainly does happen, and through the years there have been plenty of legitimate (and illegitimate) lawsuits claiming copyright infringement. Some songwriters have fallen into a trap of the so-called poor man's copyright in order to supposedly protect their songs cheaply (see "In the Mix" in this chapter to learn more about this subject).

In the Mix: The "Poor Man's Copyright"

Somewhere along the way in the history of music, some enterprising (and evidently poor) soul decided that mailing a copy of his or her song and/or lyric to him- or herself via registered mail could substitute for official copyright registration. The thinking was (and is by those who still practice it to this day) that if the song's ownership were ever contested, producing the unopened envelope would—*voilà!*—be evidence that the songwriter could claim ownership of the work based on the date of the postmark.

While it sounds like a convincing plan that would persuade a judge and jury, there are many attorneys who believe the poor man's copyright is not worth the trip to the post office or even the price of a stamp. This is because only copyright registration with the U.S. Copyright Office provides a public record of an author's claim of ownership, as well as the copyright benefits, including the following:

- A work must be registered prior to its author or publisher instituting legal action to defend it from unauthorized use.
- Copyright registration made before or within five years of a work's publication may be used as *prima facie* evidence (meaning it is presumed to be true unless disproved by evidence to the contrary) in a court of law to establish the validity of a copyright, as well as the statements affirmed on the application (such as authorship).
- Under specified circumstances, the owner of a registered copyright may be entitled to additional money in the form of statutory damages or attorney's fees in the event that infringement is proven.[*]

So unless you're a desperately down-on-your-luck songwriter eating pork and beans at every meal, you're better off having your song properly registered with the Copyright Office (when registration is appropriate, as described in this chapter) by a reputable music publisher (or by yourself, if you so choose).

[*]U.S. Copyright Office, https://www.copyright.gov/.

THE COPY *RIGHTS*

The Copyright Act of 1976 laid out the "bundle of rights" that belong to the creator of the original work. These "five rights" are the ultimate foundation upon which the creator of an original work stands:

1. To reproduce the work.
2. To prepare derivative works based upon the work.
3. To distribute copies of the work to the public by sale or other transfer of ownership, or by rental, lease, or lending.
4. To perform the work publicly.
5. To display the copyrighted work publicly.[6]

These rights are not unlimited, however. "Fair use" and other specific limitations are a part of the Copyright Act as well.

The fair use doctrine is a defense against copyright infringement when the user of a copyrighted piece has used it for the purposes of criticism, news reporting, teaching, and research. Parody can also be included as a form of fair use. Artist Weird Al Yankovic made a career out of parody songs, thus sidestepping the copyright law through the parody/fair use provision. However, Yankovic has stated that he always asks permission to do a parody song from the original recording artist of the song.[7] There are further exceptions to the copyright monopoly, and these involve what are called *compulsory licenses.*

> Under section 115 of the Copyright Act, an individual or entity, subject to certain terms and conditions, may make and distribute phonorecords of nondramatic musical works that have been distributed as phonorecords to the public in the United States under the authority of the copyright owner. As discussed below, this compulsory license includes the right to authorize others to engage in the making and distribution of phonorecords and to distribute the phonorecord by means of a digital phonorecord delivery.[8]

Compulsory licenses don't mean that the copyright law is to be ignored; they just mean that a copyright owner is *required* to issue a license to someone who wants to use the work (although the user of the copyrighted work can't alter the fundamental nature of the original work without permission).

The five compulsory licenses are:

1. Cable television rebroadcast
2. Public Broadcasting System

3. Jukeboxes
4. Digital performance of records
5. Phonorecords and digital downloads of nondramatic musical compositions. (A *phonorecord* as defined by the law is any sort of recording these days . . . not just an old-fashioned vinyl record.)[9]

COPYRIGHT REGISTRATION

As discussed earlier, my opinion is to let a reputable music publisher take care of registering a copyright for your song after you have assigned the copyright to the publisher when you have decided that your song is "safe" with that publisher. (Read about how to select a publisher in chapter 6.) But if you choose to register your song with the Copyright Office in Washington, DC, you do so by completing an application for copyright registration. Such a registration can be done through the U.S. Copyright Office website's registration portal (www.copyright.gov) or by doing so physically through U.S. mail. Such registration contains three essential elements: "a completed application form, a nonrefundable filing fee ($$), and a nonreturnable deposit—that is, a copy or copies of the work being registered and 'deposited' with the Copyright Office."[10]

For general information about copyright, call the Copyright Public Information Office at (202) 707-3000 or (877) 476-0778 (toll free). Staff members are on duty from 8:30 a.m. to 5:00 p.m., eastern time, Monday through Friday, except for federal holidays. Recorded information is available 24 hours a day. To request paper application forms or circulars, call (202) 707-9100 and leave a message. By regular mail, write to the Library of Congress Copyright Office–PUB 101 Independence Avenue, SE Washington, DC 20559.

THE COPYRIGHT NOTICE

After all this talk about protecting one's songs, it's interesting to note that U.S. law no longer requires a copyright notice (remember . . . your piece is copyrighted as long as it's in a "fixed, tangible form"). However, placing a notice on your work is beneficial.

The actual, basic notice should contain these three elements:

1. The symbol © (letter C in a circle)
2. The year of first publication

3. The name of the copyright owner[11]
  Example: © 2018 John Doe

A phonorecord copyright notice substitutes a letter *P* in a circle instead of a *C*, since a master recording of a song is a separate, copyrightable entity from the actual song itself.[12] For example, someone can own the recording of a song (the "master") but not the song itself. As a further example, in the case of the Acme Record Company that makes a recording of John Doe's song (titled "I Love Music"), the notice on the recording would be as follows:

I LOVE MUSIC
© 2018 John Doe
℗ Acme Records

A preference by many companies is to give slightly more embellishment on a copyright notice:

© Copyright 2018 by John Doe. All Rights Reserved.

The "rights reserved," of course, are the famed "bundle of rights."

INFRINGEMENTS

Copyright infringement is simply using copyrighted works without the permission of the copyright owner. If someone uses your song, plagiarizes your song, photocopies it, records it without the proper license, and so on, that constitutes infringement. Remember, the owner of the song has a "monopoly" on its use (with the aforementioned limitations), so the song owner has the right to protect his or her intellectual property.

At its core, infringing is stealing, plain and simple. And when songs are stolen, everyone loses: the creator(s) of the song, publisher, record company, agents, attorneys, and so forth. The one(s) who are doing the stealing ultimately lose out as well, since creators of the music are dependent upon its sale for their livelihood. And when the purveyors of music can't eat, they have to go do something else! What does the owner of a song receive when their copyright is infringed upon?

1. An injunction. Go to court and stop the infringer from using the work illegally.

2. Fair market value (FMV). Whatever revenues the infringer gleaned as a result of using the song illegally, the song owner gets the fair market value of those revenues.

3. The infringer's profits. This is an alternative to receiving FMV but can be better and more desirable than FMV because the infringer may have originally garnered revenues much higher than FMV for the use of the song.

4. Statutory damages. When the song owner can't prove actual damages in dollar amounts, the owner can receive anywhere from $750 to $30,000 per infringement.[13] Willing infringements carry higher penalties; "innocent" (unknowing) infringements carry less.

5. Destruction or seizure. The illegal copies of your work can be seized and destroyed by order of a court.

6. Criminal penalties. These can be levied against the infringer when the infringement is proven to be willful.

7. Costs. The song owner can recover court costs (and even in some cases, attorney's fees).

As you can see, infringement carries a lot of ramifications with it. Unfortunately, it happens every day, so it's to the song owner's advantage to be up to speed on what can be done when infringed upon.

JOINT WORKS

You and your friend Taylor decide you're going to write a song together. So who owns the copyright? You or Taylor?

Both authors own the work. When creators work together to create a new work, with the intent of combining their creative efforts into a single work, they have created what is called a joint work. So both authors jointly own the newly created work. Unless the authors of the joint work specify otherwise, the law will divide ownership equally among the coauthors.[14]

That can mean, in the case of two coauthors, and absent an agreement to the contrary, a right to an accounting for 50 percent of the proceeds of the exploitation of a given work. As a result, it is a very good idea for the collaborators to work through their agreement, and, if they intend to split the proceeds unequally, to say so in a contract binding all the coauthors. Even when creators have contributed separate, distinct parts of the work (e.g., music or lyrics), they each own an interest in the *entire* copyright, not just their own contributions.

But what happens when one of coauthors wants to do something with the song that the other creator may disagree with? For example, Taylor wants to use the song in a beer commercial, but you think that will cheapen the value of the song. According to the Copyright Act, Taylor can deal *nonexclusively* with the *entire* composition (and have the song used in the commercial), but you must be paid for your share of the revenues from the beer commercial use.

Big takeaway regarding joint works: Make sure you're writing with a person(s) with whom you see eye to eye on how your "baby" (i.e., your song) will be exploited in the future.

WORKS FOR HIRE

If a work is work "for hire" (i.e., someone commissions an author, sculptor, or any creative person to create something), the person(s) or commissioning entity is designated as the author, even if the person(s) creating the work is given credit for doing so.[15] In this case, the work must be done by the employee within the *scope of their employment*. For example, a music editor at a publishing company may make creative changes (with the composer's permission) to a song. But those changes made by the editor were done within the scope of his or her employment. Therefore, those creative changes are "work for hire" and the editor isn't entitled to any portion of the copyright or royalty remuneration. The editor receives a salary or other remuneration from his or her employer as a means of compensation for the editor's services. The employer can be a firm, an organization, or an individual.

Works for hire need not be written by employees, however. For example, often record companies or music publishers will engage the services of a music transcriber, arranger, orchestrator, or the like to create content (or enhance existing content owned by the record company or publisher) in which the nature of the services doesn't warrant (often by industry standards) cause for a royalty to be paid to the contributor. In this case, a work for hire agreement is proffered. Many times, the contributor would rather be paid for work for hire anyway since this money is offered up front (either at the beginning of the project or upon completion of the project) and will be delivered faster than a royalty (which can take up to a year or more to receive after the completion of a project). Granted, if the project is a hit, the contributor would have done better off receiving a royalty. But the reverse is also true: If the project is a bomb, the contributor would have received very little royalty on the "back end," making up-front work-for-hire money a better bet. Sometimes contributors don't have a choice on whether or not remuneration will be work for hire versus a royalty, but when they do, they should choose based on their current situation (and willingness to take a risk). Do they need the cash now (and therefore agree to a work-for-hire agreement), or can they afford to hope the project is successful and wait for remuneration (and therefore agree to a royalty scenario)? Therein lies the rub! But with industry experience (and/or guidance from another trusted advisor), contributors have a good chance of making the right choice.

Music copyright is a complex issue with numerous facets and nuances. This chapter contains the essential aspects of this foundational element of the music business. To learn more, go to www.copyright.gov.

NOTES

1. "Press Laws," *1902 Encyclopedia*, http://www.1902encyclopedia.com/.

2. U.S. Copyright Office, "The 18th Century," Timeline, Copyright.gov, https://www.copyright.gov/timeline/timeline_18th_century.html.

3. "Berne Convention," Wikipedia, https://en.wikipedia.org/wiki/Berne_Convention.

4. U.S. Copyright Office, *Duration of Copyright*, Circular 15a (Washington, DC: U.S. Government Printing Office, 2011), https://www.copyright.gov/circs/circ15a.pdf.

5. U.S. Copyright Office, *Copyright Basics*, Circular 1 (Washington, DC: U.S. Government Printing Office, 2017), https://www.copyright.gov/circs/circ01.pdf.

6. U.S. Copyright Office, *Copyright Basics*.

7. Geoff Edgers, "Was 'Weird Al' the Real Star All Along? After Nearly 40 Years of Parodying Celebrities, the Accordion-Playing Nerd Has Become a Legend in His Own Right," *Washington Post*, February 16, 2017.

8. U.S. Copyright Office, *Compulsory License for Making and Distributing Phonorecord*, Circular 73 (Washington, DC: U.S. Government Printing Office, 2018), https://www.copyright.gov/circs/circ73.pdf.

9. U.S. Copyright Office, *Compulsory License*.

10. U.S. Copyright Office, *Copyright Registration*, Circular 2 (Washington, DC: U.S. Government Printing Office, 2017), https://www.copyright.gov/circs/circ02.pdf.

11. U.S. Copyright Office, *Copyright Basics*.

12. U.S. Copyright Office, *Copyright Basics*.

13. Pam Phillips and Andrew Surmani, *Copyright Handbook for Music Educators and Directors: A Practical, Easy-to-Read Guide* (Van Nuys, CA: Alfred Music, 2017).

14. Subcommittee on Patents, Trademarks, and Copyrights, U.S. Senate Committee on the Judiciary, *Copyright Law Revision: Studies 11–13*, study 12, *Joint Ownership of*

Copyrights (Washington, DC: U.S. Government Printing Office, 1960), https://www.copyright.gov/history/studies/study12.pdf.

15. U.S. Copyright Office, *Works Made for Hire*, Circular 9 (Washington, DC: U.S. Government Printing Office, 2012), https://www.copyright.gov/circs/circ09.pdf.

4

BAND ON THE RUN

A Career in Performance

Being in the audience actually looks like quite a lot of fun.

—Paul McCartney

Even legendary artist Paul McCartney (cowriter of the iconic, chart-topping song "Band on the Run" and, of course, one of the Beatles) acknowledged the rigors of being on the stage and road with the above statement, with a seeming longing to sit back and enjoy the show himself now and then. But as noted previously, the music business "machine" requires a great deal of different types of people to make it hum. *And someone has to make the music!* You may be one of the people making the music. And even if you aren't and instead want to be on the business side of the music business, it behooves you to understand the ins and outs and ups and downs of the life of a performer.

There are several pros and cons to starting a band versus joining one (more on joining one later). But one of the main advantages of starting your own band is that the vision can (and must) be yours. Then it's up to you to find others who share that vision and will buy into it to help it be realized. More on vision later.

"LET'S START A BAND!"

The list of legendary bands could fill several pages in this book: the Who, Green Day, Fleetwood Mac, Aerosmith, the Rolling Stones, Radiohead, Pink Floyd, AC/DC, Pearl Jam, the Eagles, Led Zeppelin, the Beatles . . . and on the list could go. Somewhere along the way for each of them, someone had the idea to start making music as a group. The lure of having a legendary career like one of these bands is enough to make every 15-year-old guitar player dream of fame and fortune on the road, playing his or her music to millions of adoring fans. And that can happen.

However, the odds of becoming another legendary band aren't good. But so what? If that is your dream, you simply must pursue it. And if you play your cards right and strategize carefully, you might at least be able to make a decent living following your passions.

This isn't meant to discourage you but to give you a realistic picture of what lies ahead for someone who chooses to make music for a living (at least in the early days, and especially in today's transformed music business world).

For example, if you want to be an actor, you might not be the next Meryl Streep or George Clooney, but you can possibly at least be a working actor making a reasonable living and be able to pay the bills. Depending on your definition of success, that can be a wonderful life. The same is true with being a working musician. If you can make ends meet and live a life that is comfortable enough to follow your passions, then mission accomplished. And while you're doing that with a strategy, passion, and plan, there's certainly a chance you just might hit the big time. As the Roman philosopher Seneca said, "Luck is what happens when preparation meets opportunity."

The upside of forming your own band is that you have the creative control and assurance that you'll be playing music you enjoy in venues you prefer. You will also control the creative direction the band takes. Creative direction of a band has broken up many legendary (and obscure, for that matter) bands. So make sure whomever you bring on board as a part of the team (and the word *team* is important in this context since you want everyone who performs with you to see it as a team effort, with you as the leader) is in agreement with your overall vision, direction, and leadership for the band. As its leader, you can also set the size of the group, style and content of what's performed, where and when you perform, and the rehearsal schedule.

The flip side of forming your own band and being its leader is that you're managing all of the responsibilities of the group until such a time as you're able to delegate those either to other trustworthy band members or a professional team (more on team building later). Those responsibilities include being the band's manager, booking agent, and promoter and handling all the contractual obligations with other band members and the venues in which you perform.

HAVE A VISION, HAVE A PLAN

As with any goal in life, to accomplish it one needs a crystal-clear mental picture as to what one is attempting to accomplish (a vision) and a step-by-step strategy as to how one is going to accomplish it (a plan). The same applies to starting a band. Countless young (and older) people jump into saying, "Let's start a band!" fueled strictly on emotion and adrenaline, with no regard as to having a clear vision and plan for how to develop a successful band. Add to that the fact that most creative types who are band members are not always known for their business savvy (although there are certainly exceptions), and this potentially sets the band up for conflicts of interest, confusion, hurt feelings, lost friendships, financial burdens, and ultimate failure. That has happened countless times, you can be sure. Naturally, you want to avoid all of these things. You can do so by not only having a clear *vision* for your band but also by having a *plan*.

As for vision, you should know (mostly instinctively) how you want your band to sound, look, and perform. How can you set your band apart with a unique sound, look, and performance? There are countless bands in the world, and your job at this stage is to determine how yours is going to stand out without being gimmicky. How can your band forge a unique niche among the sea of bands yet be an authentic, organic match for your unique, authentic, creative vision? This is a question that simply must be answered with complete clarity before you book your first gig. So take the time to do some real self-examination about the type of music that you're most passionate about and have always had the most success performing . . . when time seemed to stand still and your passion and the music were flowing freely. Most importantly, be yourself! Trust your instincts as you hone in on fine-tuning how you will express yourself artistically. That's the fun part. The harder part (at least for many, as noted above) is the business side of things.

ART VERSUS COMMERCE: THIS IS A BUSINESS

After you have gained complete clarity on your vision for the band, the equally important foundation of your strategy should be a business plan. If you start your band knowing that it is first and foremost a business, then you're on the right track. I'm not talking about a classic business plan where cash flow is projected along with EBITDA (earnings before interest, tax, depreciation, and amortization) . . . although such a plan would be a fine idea for a beginning band. The basic business plan you should have involves selecting a team to support the band. This is one of the most important business decisions you'll make to help assure your short-, medium-, and long-term future (whether or not you remain with the same band and team down the road).

Many beginning artists choose the DIY (do-it-yourself) option these days (and forego a traditional business team per se) since record labels aren't quite as powerful as they once were with the decline of physical CD sales. That said, most artists of today still hold to the traditional model of finding a team and landing a recording deal with a major or minor label. If you choose this route, the members of your team should be:

1. Personal manager
2. Attorney
3. Business manager
4. Agent

Another tip: Most beginning and emerging bands indeed "do it them-selves" in the early stages. (Besides, when you're starting out, how can you afford to pay a personal manager right out of the gate?) But at some point in their career, based on their growth and achievements with their number of gigs, fan base, and so on, they reach out to hire a personal manager. And if further success and revenue warrant it, their team can expand.

PERSONAL MANAGER

The division of labor in the artist/manager relationship is to allow artists to concentrate on writing and recording songs, rehearsing and perform-ing live shows, and growing and engaging their fan base, while managers analyze data and make strategic recommendations based on the information gathered. Therefore, the manager's role today is less that of an advocate and motivator and more that of an analyst and advisor.

In today's music business equation, personal managers have a variety of resources at their disposal: BigChampagne, Bandcamp, Next Big Sound, and other media-measurement tools help them analyze data to determine vital bits of information, such as:

- Which of the artists' products sell the most (downloads, physical products, custom items, tickets, subscriptions, etc.) and which sell the least and perhaps should be discontinued

- What new products can be added and which new revenue streams can be exploited
- Which pay models work the best (fixed price, pay what you want, donations, bundles, etc.)
- Which campaigns are the most effective (virtual street teams, newsletters, videos, chats, vlogs, blogs, etc.) and which ones generate the most feedback and results
- Which calls-to-action are the most effective (e.g., sign up for the mailing list for a free download, preorder a limited edition, autographed CD)
- What trends or patterns are developing and how to best take advantage of them
- Which platforms/widgets are most useful and relevant for a particular artist (review demos and sign up for trials to find the best fit)
- Which songs, videos, images, T-shirt designs, and so on resonate with fans the most
- Who the artists' "superfans" are and how to leverage that relationship to generate more sales
- Which questions to include in polls to figure out what the artists' fans want
- In which ways fans most wish to engage and interact with the artist
- Where are fans clustered and what are the best ways to route a tour
- What does the data reveal that will result in an increase in sales and income
- What are the true costs of the artist's operations (i.e., what is being earned vs. what is being spent)
- And much more

While some bands can—and do—perform many of the above tasks themselves, there's often a price to pay when and if they do. Even after your band is up and running, acting as your own manager can leave the band no time to do what bands should do most: rehearse, record, perform, interact with fans, write, and so forth. This can lead to burnout and discouragement when too many irons are in the fire and things don't always go right.

The best managers cover all these bases and free up the band to do what they do best. The manager should have a complete and in-depth understanding of how all these pieces fit together and be able to guide the band in all these areas. The end result is not only a happier and more successful band but one that is profitable, because remember . . . this is a business.

How to find a personal manager? If you've got your act together (literally) in the areas of finance, booking, online presence, and fan-base management on a small level, then personal managers will often find *you*. But if you want to shop around, your network of fellow bands who do have managers is a great place to start. Searching the Internet is certainly a viable path to finding names/companies who provide management services. One major pitfall to avoid is having a parent or relative serve as your personal manager. They're most likely instantly and permanently positively biased toward you and your band, and it's naturally hard for that person to be objective about your career and the right moves for you. It's not a bad thing to have input from family and friends who care for you (those with the most common sense and a track record of success to back up their words), but they still are unlikely to have had a music business background that qualifies them to offer you sound advice in this area.

ATTORNEY

Some bands procure an attorney before they use the services of anyone else listed as a team member. This is because even when forming a band, it's often a good idea to solidify several key issues before getting too far down the road. For example:

1. Who owns what and in what percentage if the band breaks up (e.g., the name of the band, the band's website, fan-base list, profits)?
2. How are artistic decisions handled (e.g., is it an equal democracy or does a particular member or members have greater voting power)?
3. How are business decisions addressed (e.g., when and where to tour, how much to spend on recordings, if and when a band member is fired)?

These are just a few of the very important decisions that come up regularly, and how these things will be handled needs to be addressed early on. An experienced music business attorney can help you address these vitally important issues up front, at the beginning of the band's existence. That's the time to do it, before things get complicated and busy (and you certainly want them to get busy but not complicated from a legal standpoint).

Attorneys are arguably the most important member of your team, since by the nature of their job, they are more connected with a wider variety of people in the music business (provided they specialize in the music business, and it's recommended that when you hire an attorney you use one that does indeed specialize in the music business). The reason attorneys are generally more connected is that they often have a number of clients in several areas of the music business; therefore, they may be able to connect you with other helpful people in the business (such as publishers, managers, and record label representatives).

You will also want to select an attorney whose personal style is a match for you and the band. For example, some attorneys are more casual and "laid back" and want to make you feel as if they are one of you. Others can be much more rigid and businesslike and want just the facts. Either type is fine as long as he or she is a competent lawyer; it's just a matter of your personal preference as to which you select to represent you. And as for how to determine whether or not the attorney is competent, the process is somewhat like having your car fixed if you know nothing about cars. You check out his or her references, listen carefully to the person's answers on how to fix things, see if it makes sense to you, and so on. You can also talk to some current clients before committing to the attorney to make sure you are comfortable before hiring him or her. Attorneys can be very expensive, so you don't want to waste money on one who makes big promises to bring you fame and fortune and then delivers nothing. (Right off the bat beware of any attorney who promises you "fame and fortune.") The music business is full of fast-talking, smooth attorneys who will take your money quickly in the form of a retainer (money up front) and deliver absolutely nothing in return (other than a lot of feel-good rhetoric and empty promises). Bottom line: Do your due diligence as noted above to try to avoid wasted money, time, and added frustration.

BUSINESS MANAGER

A business manager handles primarily one thing for you: money! This is the person on your team who takes care of collecting the money, tracking its incoming and outgoing movement (i.e., handling your accounts payable and receivable), helping file tax returns (or doing the filing for you), investing your money, and so forth. The music business landscape is littered with major and minor players who entrusted this key role to someone whom they eventually found was untrustworthy, perhaps stole from them, and they now have the financial (and emotional) scars to prove it. So suffice it to say that you should take plenty of time and research potential business managers *carefully* before you give anyone the keys to your financial kingdom, even if your kingdom is tiny at the beginning. As with any member of your team, ask for references, then check them(!). Ask for a list of current clients, and then talk to several of them to see if they're happy with the service they're getting.

Preferably, your business manager will be a CPA (certified public accountant). CPAs go through stringent requirements to earn that certification, and having a business manager who is a competent CPA will give you the assurance that your money is being handled professionally, legally, efficiently, and effectively.

Other things to look for in a business manager:

1. *A degree in business administration.* This will only enhance his or her knowledge of tax laws, investments, accounting, and even negotiating.
2. *Reporting approach.* What sorts of financial reporting will the business manager provide for you based on how much you're paying him or her? (More on payment later.) For example, a monthly P&L (profit and loss) statement for your band should be standard. You simply must know if you're making or losing money. Will your business manager help walk you through the P&Ls so that you can understand such reports? And will he or she be patient and noncondescending if you ask some dumb questions? (There are ultimately no dumb questions asked by artists of their business managers. The business part of the music business is this person's specialty, and he or she should be part teacher when patiently and clearly explaining any complex financial reports to you, which you're paying him or her to provide for you.)
3. *Related representation.* Does he or she represent other bands, solo artists, writers, and so on? The music business has its quirks and nuances unlike other conventional businesses, and having a business manager who's acquainted with the ins and outs of the music business is very important.
4. *Level of involvement.* At larger management firms, your representative will sometimes farm the lesser accounting tasks out to someone else in the firm. That can be a great idea if he or she is saving you money by having a junior member of his or her staff (whose hourly rate is less than the business manager's) take care of some of the accounting functions of your account. But you want to make sure you're not getting the short end of the stick and being relegated to paying more for less.
5. *Checks and balances.* This isn't referring to writing checks and monitoring your bank balance (although those are also very im-

portant functions of a business manager) but making sure you have a system in place where you can't get ripped off by this person. For example, perhaps you're the only person who can sign checks. That doesn't mean this person couldn't forge your signature, but if you—or another trusted person on your team—is looking at the canceled checks to make sure it's your authentic signature on them, that helps ensure your money isn't being embezzled. It's happened countless times before, and you needn't be a victim of such potentially financially ruinous activities.

6. *A manner with which you're comfortable.* As with your other team members, you need someone with whom you're going to connect and feel comfortable. If you can build a great rapport with this person, that will give you both a path to open communication and honesty.

Another important consideration: Does this person carry errors and omissions (E&O) insurance? Such insurance is common in many businesses, but in your case it will help protect you if your business manager mismanages your finances.

As for paying a business manager, most work for either a percentage of your revenues (generally in the 5 percent range), a flat fee, or an hourly rate. When the business manager is taking a percentage of your earnings, most do not require money up front (although some may as an advance against their future earnings). Some work on a combination of these approaches. Again, don't be afraid to ask "dumb" questions (but remember, there are none!) of this person so that you can get a clear understanding as to how he or she will be remunerated and build that into your budget (which he or she will help you construct).

AGENT

An agent is a luxury for beginning bands, and if the band has a personal manager, the role of an agent becomes even more limited. If you have a personal manager, the agent generally interacts with that person more than with you. The primary role of the agent is to handle booking concert appearances. He or she may also be involved in booking other things such as broadcast appearances, tour sponsorships, and endorsements. But the personal manager is still in the loop on these things (as would be the band's attorney and business manager, most likely). The agent is the "fire starter" that helps make these things happen.

Agents are sometimes independent but are often found in (surprise!) agencies, such as William Morris Endeavor (WME). WME is one of the largest agencies in the world, and just as there are pros and cons to signing with a large music publisher versus a small, independent one, there are similar advantages and disadvantages to signing on with a very large agency versus a small one. It's ultimately up to you, of course, and how you're "wired" as to which direction you choose. But again, relationships and reputation are top considerations.

Regarding remuneration for an agent, they generally work on a 10 percent basis since the unions put a cap on how much they can charge. There are some exceptions to this cap as regards personal appearances through American Federation of Musicians (AFM) guidelines. Consult the AFM, your attorney, or your personal manager for when such an exception might take effect.

IF YOU CAN'T BEAT 'EM, JOIN 'EM!

But what if you don't want to start your own band and instead just want to join an existing, established one (either through invitation or audition)? Joining an existing band certainly has its advantages over starting your own. However, you won't have the creative control you may desire, let alone fulfill a vision you have for the group. These are trade-offs you'll have to weigh. Some musicians get their feet wet by playing in an established band for a while, learning the ropes, then branching out on their own after a few years or more. There is no single path to success and fulfillment.

By joining an existing band, you could potentially be working with musicians from whom you can learn a lot and have a steadier income stream faster. Watching others perform who (most likely) have been doing it longer than you also has its advantages. An established band will also probably have long-standing relationships with attorneys, managers, and so on, and you can learn from those relationships as well.

Once again, there's a flip side: You can't select your fellow bandmates, and you'll have very little (if any) creative control. Once you're hired and have signed a contract, you'll be part of the band's "family" and learn that there may be internal creative conflicts (large or small) that you'll have to deal with . . . or you may decide you can't handle it and then try to get out (there certainly should be an exit clause in your contract).

FINDING THAT BAND

If you would like to join a band but don't immediately have a connection with one that you know is looking for another member, there are websites and other online means (e.g., social media) of connecting with the right group. Groups who are looking to replace a departing band member often reach out on social media for that replacement, but you can be proactive as well. Here are the questions you need to answer before you start looking around:

1. What sort of sound will be right for you? If possible, have some samples of your work to share with a potential band so they'll know immediately what your capabilities are.
2. How hard do you want to work? And how much time can you afford to devote to the band? If you're a full-time student with a part-time job, that doesn't leave much time for rehearsals and performances. But perhaps you can quit your part-time job if you get the position with the band. When you connect with a potential band, make sure you know how much of a time commitment is involved. A companion question to this one is, "How hard will you be expected to work?," meaning not only how much time commitment is expected, as just noted, but also how difficult is the music you will be expected to perform? (And are you up to it?) Will you be spending countless hours outside of rehearsals just so you can keep up?
3. How successful is this band? Do all the due diligence possible (talk to venues where the band has appeared, check out their website, ask questions of anyone who's acquainted with them, etc.) to find out where this band stands in their career development. You don't want to board a sinking ship. Also, if you're replacing an existing band member, why did that band member leave (or were they fired)? How long has the band been in existence? How is it structured? (Who makes all the decisions? Is it one person or do band members have a say in its governance? If so, how much?)
4. What might the future hold? In other words, what is the leader's vision for the future for this band? Does he or she just want to focus on local, area, or regional gigs, or does the leader have visions of a national or international scope? Has the band made any recordings, and, if not, is that in the future plan for the group? Recordings are a major commitment of time (and money) for all concerned, and you need to know up front what might be in the offing for that aspect of things.

BAND-AIDS

Now we shift gears to give tips for when you're the one doing the hiring of a potential new band member. As with any new hire, you want to *make sure the person is a great fit for your group*. Otherwise, you're potentially setting yourself and the band up for a possibly painful experience if you eventually have to fire the person. So here are five "band-aids" for avoiding those pitfalls:

    1. *Audition.* Of course, before you hire a new member for your presumably tightly knit group, have him or her sit in on a few rehearsals and make music with you. This is akin to dating before marriage, and just about anyone can sustain a good attitude dur-

Fig 4.1.   Find the Right Band Member. *Illustration by Richard Duszczak*

ing a date. It's a few months or years later that the problems arise. But if there's been an ample dating period, potential problems will usually reveal themselves (and how such problems are handled is important too). The same is true of a potential band member after having that person participate in several (you decide how many) rehearsals with the group. You'll get an instant sense of the chemistry among the existing members and the "newbie." Plus, you'll figure out pretty fast if he or she can keep up musically and mesh well with your form of rehearsals. If the person fares well in rehearsals, a trial performance isn't a bad idea at all before hiring the person and officially signing him or her up. Once the potential member has proven him- or herself, that person will be all the more appreciative of being asked to become a part of your group.

2. *Good work ethic.* Being in a band requires commitment and a good work ethic. This includes showing up on time and consistently, being prepared, and having a positive attitude, ready to make music. The positive attitude part can't be underscored enough. That said, we're all human and "life happens" from time to time. But being late to rehearsal or being consistently moody or aloof doesn't lend itself to a positive vibe for the group, especially if it's a small group. One bad apple can spoil the bunch if you're not careful, and you don't have time to waste in ironing out someone's personal problems during rehearsal. Musicians are notoriously emotional beings . . . that's what helps make us tick! But don't let those emotions—from any of your band members—rule the day. This is part of solid management to keep the band on track and headed in the right direction without distractions.

3. *Stage presence.* Let's face it . . . a band is full of performers, and the audience is there to be entertained! Stage presence is one of those things that you sort of have or you don't. Sure, there are things you can to do improve it and enhance it (and books have been written about that), and the more experience one has in front of people, the better. But there is that intangible "wow" factor that you can sense from someone even in rehearsal, and you can tell if that person is good at naturally emoting and communicating through music to an audience. Be on the lookout for that element in a potential new band member and determine if that person can contribute to what I call a "high EQ" (entertainment quotient).

4. *Talent.* Don't settle for mediocrity. Look for someone who will bring excellence to your group. And if that person has a great attitude, as

noted before, you won't have to worry about him or her copping an attitude about how much more talented he or she is than other members of the band (if indeed that even happens to be the truth). There's nothing worse than someone with mediocre talent (or incredible talent) who thinks they're the next Beyoncé.

5. *It's a wrap.* You may be fortunate enough to have several people from which to choose. Be professional in calling each of those who auditioned, but call the person who won the position first. That way, if that person has had a change of heart and decided he or she is not interested (for whatever reason), you can fall back on the person who was your second (though acceptable) choice.

GET YOUR GROOVE ON

There are countless bands out there of every shape and size, and as noted earlier, very few of them make it to the big time. But first things first. There's the small time, the medium time, the big time, and the medium-small time . . . and so on. If you're just starting out, you should be happy to get decent gigs anywhere. Here are tips to provide a good launching pad for your band:

1. *Get a great name.* A name for your band is one of the first items of business, obviously. A great band name is memorable, original, and catchy. Panic! At the Disco, Coldplay, Hootie and the Blowfish, and Red Hot Chili Peppers come to mind as ones that certainly fit the bill. Have fun and take your time coming up with a name that is significant to you, thrills you, and feels right.

2. *Have a unified sound.* Although sounding great and unified (in tune!) is certainly a musical consideration, what this item concerns is having a clear vision on how you want your band to sound and the material you're going to perform. Will you perform cover songs only? New material only? A mix of those two? That's up to you, but it's important to send a clear message regarding who you are and what you're about musically. Your band's name can also possibly reflect this aspect of your group.

3. *Brand your band.* Through the years, various bands have had distinctive looks to rise above the crowd. The Beatles did it with longer hair way back in the 1960s in an era when hair on males was short. Other groups have set themselves apart with certain

colors or clothing styles (e.g., all band members wear coats and ties). First and foremost, the music and sound of these bands had to be distinct, but having a different look made them all the more memorable and marketable. See "In the Mix" in this chapter for more information on the important aspect of branding.

4. *Rehearse with purpose.* As the old joke goes, when someone stops a person on the streets of New York City and asks, "How do I get to Carnegie Hall?," the person responds, "Practice, man, practice!" Not only should your rehearsals be consistent and planned, but they should be purposeful and focused. Have specific goals for each rehearsal regarding what you want/need to accomplish. Don't keep them open-ended. Have an agreed-upon starting and stopping time. Respect your band's personal time.

Once you've indeed "gotten your groove on" with these basic steps in your band's development, you're ready for your first gig. Choose the venue, music set, date, and time carefully. The last thing you want for your premiere appearance is to have the audience walking away wanting less. You want them to want more! They should be buzzing about what an exciting time it was and asking when your next gig will be. And if you're short on gigs, you can check out sites such as www.sonicbids.com, www.indieonthemove .com, and www.getthatgig.com, which are designed to connect you with promoters, help you book more gigs, and help grow your career.

In the Mix: Band Branding

Aside from sounding fabulous and putting on a great show, branding your band is probably the most important thing you'll do to contribute to your future success.

First, develop a website as soon as possible and read up on SEO (search engine optimization) to maximize your exposure. Starting a website in today's world can be relatively easy and inexpensive, but getting a large number of people to discover it is difficult without maximum SEO so that you will pop up on as many searches as possible. Become an expert on SEO. Facebook, Twitter, Instagram, and other existing and emerging forms of social media are your best friends when marketing your band these days, so use those platforms to their maximum potential (and spend money in that area carefully and wisely). Use your website and all social media to develop an active email list of fans, and then communicate with those fans on a regular basis. You need to connect with those fans consistently so that they will in turn connect and relate to what you're doing.

That said, here are the "10 Commandments" of band branding:

1. *Have a great and memorable logo.* Logos can be expensive if created by a professional designer, so if you can't find an affordable designer, consider asking a university design student who might do it for you at a very reasonable price (or even for free just to get something for their résumé).
2. *Be consistent.* Make your website layout and design consistent with your band's aesthetic (and free from clutter).
3. *Say something with your fashion choices.* Color choice and coordination, fabrics, and overall style (e.g., gritty or glamorous) all will make a nonverbal statement about who your band is. And again, the message you send should be consistent with your overall branding plan.
4. *Take cool band photos.* Use a professional photographer if possible, but if not, with today's cell phones, you can get high-quality photos for free.
5. *Create amazing CD packaging.* Look closely at your favorite band's packaging for inspiration (not to rip off their ideas). Think, "Would I like this packaging if I saw it on a merchandise table or in a retail store?" Make your packaging distinctive somehow.
6. *Do a vinyl release.* Vinyl records have and are continuing to make a comeback, and releasing your recording in vinyl format will really make a bold and fun statement about your band.
7. *Conduct free giveaways through your website, newsletter, and social media platforms.*
8. *Blog.* Connecting with your fan base is of the utmost importance, and sharing your thoughts in a blog (posted on all your social media platforms) is a great way to connect.
9. *Shoot a music video that is worth sharing.* Again, check out some of your favorite bands' videos and analyze what makes the videos great and memorable. Find a video expert to help you make it happen.
10. *Sell T-shirts and merch.* By getting your fans to buy merchandise, you further connect with them when they're not at one of your concerts or listening to your recordings. These pieces of merch also act as free advertising for your band courtesy of the user of the merch.

AVOID THESE SOUR NOTES

Those are some *dos* to starting your band . . . now here are some classic *don'ts*:

1. *Choosing with tunnel vision.* Musical skills are naturally very important, but they not the only criteria by which you should choose your band members. Choosing musicians who are well rounded is more important . . . that is, band members who are communicative onstage and off, responsible, dependable, and who are team members is most important.

2. *Not being a clear leader.* If it's your band, then lead the band. Although you may have a clear vision about what you want your sound and look to be, that's not enough. First and foremost, you need to be able to communicate that vision to your fellow band members, and if you are passionate about it and that vision resonates with them, they will follow and be a part of that clear vision. But you also need to lead the band in all other ways: financially, creatively, and so on.

3. *Being unfocused.* If your band is all over the board musically, you're not going to communicate a unified message to your audience. Plus, it will be difficult for radio programmers (both traditional and nontraditional radio) to find a spot for you in their lineup. Creative freedom is wonderful, but don't dilute your branding by not having a clear focus musically.

4. *Being impatient.* It's important that you realize success doesn't happen overnight (and you should remind your band of that if you're the leader). Success is generally achieved through countless achievements and breaks that build up over time. The band's morale can ebb and flow based on different gigs, but it's up to the leader to help the band keep the big picture in mind (and to know what that big picture is to begin with) and to keep positive morale alive. If you're happy being a local, working cover band . . . then great. If you want to be the next big thing and perform on national television, that's another thing. Either goal is fine, but you must help pace your band's expectations accordingly with a realistic time frame in which to achieve your goals.

5. *Having a poor or no website.* Social media, although extremely important, is no substitute for a great website. Not only should you have

a fully functioning website that is easy to navigate, but you should spend some money on boosting your search engine presence and take time to review your analytics.

FAN THE FAN FLAMES!

When starting a new band, your fan base is nonexistent. And one of the first questions from a potential record label who is considering signing you is going to be, "How large is your fanbase?"

So how does a new band go about building that fan base?

Obviously, the aforementioned social media and website are the major tools. But there are other important ways to "fan the fan flames" to generate some "heat" for your band:

1. *Local networking.* The town in which your band is based (regardless of its size) is loaded with other musicians. Be it music teachers, other bands, solo musicians, you name it . . . they're there. Perhaps you were in your high school band or chorus or the church choir. Today's legendary performers often got their start performing in their local church choir or high school band. Musicians talk to each other and make music with each other. Reach out to as many as possible in your immediate area to let them know what you're doing with your band. Most likely, they will be able to recommend your band for gigs and help get a good buzz going about it.

2. *Be everywhere.* As you network and get gigs, make sure your band's name and logo are as visible as possible in as many logical places as possible. When you get a gig, work hard to put posters (yes, posters) up around town . . . in addition to all the website and social media work you'll do to promote your appearance. Encourage your musician friends (including fellow bands with whom you've connected through your networking activities) to promote your show (and likewise promote theirs for them). Also, if your town (or one nearby) is large enough, it may have open mic nights at a local club. Do it! Gain all the exposure you can to keep generate a positive buzz. Finally, most towns . . . even the small ones . . . often have some sort of public street fair in the spring, summer, or fall. Work to get included on one of those events, where people can see you for free and fall in love with what you're doing (and then tell others).

3. *Reach out.* Depending on the size of your market (local town), you may have to go to adjacent cities so that you're not playing the same venues over and over (and therefore not expanding your fan base). There's nothing inherently wrong with a steady gig at a local hotel's restaurant or lounge, but be careful that you don't get too comfortable (and lazy) and not reach out for new fans. Again, it depends on the goal of your group as to where you play and how often. But if you want to grow your fan base, you need to strategically and carefully plan your appearances (from a geographic and frequency perspective). If that means a bit of regional travel now and then, so be it. It can pay off in the long run.

4. *You need YouTube.* Producing a video is more inexpensive than ever before these days. Posting one of yours on YouTube can be a very powerful way to exponentially grow your fan base since as your YouTube videos (and viewings) rack up, so do your followers on YouTube, social media, web traffic, concert attendance, and so forth. Check out services such as TubeMogul or Stageit, which offer great ideas and platforms for building loyalty.

5. *Make merch!* There's no better way for your fans to connect with your message, music, and brand than if they're wearing it, drinking from a cup with your logo emblazoned on it, and so on. But don't go out and spend any money up front on creating merchandise that is only going to sit in your basement for years to come, collecting dust. You won't sell a lot of merch in the early days, but you'll sell some. And if your band grows to great heights, you'll be selling a lot of merch. But even in the early days (especially in the early days), there are affordable ways to have merch available to help not only grow but enrich your fan base (with very little or no money up front). So check out websites such as zazzle.com or dizzyjam.com. These companies specialize in helping bands and other entities create and sell custom T-shirts and other items. Turn to chapter 9 to learn more about developing and profiting from merchandising.

6. *What's in it for them?* There are even marketing tools out there that incentivize your fans to share your music. Check out FanDistro (www.fandistro.com), which helps artists spread their music virally. FanDistro enables you to reward your fans with free downloads and merch when they get a number of their friends on Facebook to download or share your music (which they call *distroing*). For example, if one of your fans introduces your music to fifteen of his or her friends via Facebook (who in turn become your fans), that

fan is rewarded with a free T-shirt. The platform is free provided you exceed earnings of $9.99 per year (easy to do!).

7. *Roll those rocks.* Finally, turn over additional "rocks" in your community and area to broaden your networking reach: Local radio stations, although busy and not necessarily inclined to automatically offer exposure to a local band, can become friends. If you make them aware of what you're doing and drop off a copy of your first recording (even if it's only one song), they may like it and put it on the air. Don't force yourself on them, but if you're professional and cordial and present you and your band in a positive, friendly way, they may like you and what you're doing and give you some on-air exposure. Some radio stations take pride in "discovering" bands for their listeners and being on the ground floor of a new band; that way if the band hits it big someday, the station and/or DJ can say, "I knew them when they were nobodies, and we helped give them their start!"

Also, don't forget local bloggers, reviewers, and (daresay) newspapers! Newspapers are still around as of this writing, and even though their readership skews older, it's one more rock to turn over in your unending quest to spread the word about your band. (And newspapers come in several forms . . . not just the local daily one, but there are a lot of local print papers and magazines selling real estate, antiques, and other things that have a "what's hot" or "what to do this weekend" section. Figure out a way to get your next gig listed in those publications. Readership of those vehicles remains solid and in some cases is growing.)

BAND ON THE RUN . . . LITERALLY!

This chapter opened with a reference to Paul McCartney and the hit song recorded by his band Wings. But as you can see, to have a successful band in this day and age (or in any age, really), it takes an enormous amount of hard work, planning, ambition, drive, creativity, hustle, luck, and more to make it successful. You are literally "on the run" to make it happen. And this may be in addition to your day job (at least at first)! But the potential rewards will be worth it. Only you and your band can define what success will be. But in the midst of all of the running, don't forget that you're making music and delivering a "product" that has the power to change lives. Or at least to make the audience forget their troubles for an evening and reflect on the gift and power of that moment and the shared experience of being moved by something that is indescribable and larger than ourselves.

5

YOU CAN BE A STAR

Being a Solo Artist

The artist is nothing without the gift, but the gift is nothing without work.

—Prince

The late, legendary solo artist Prince knew firsthand about what he spoke. His work ethic is famous among those who knew him best.

Ideally, talent walks hand in hand with a good work ethic. When the two are intertwined, good things can happen. But the music business is filled with extremely talented artists who went nowhere fast because either they weren't willing to put in the hard work required to succeed or underestimated the amount required. In either case, without hard work to back up the talent (and vice versa), the end result can be disappointment in the least and at most leading a life of "what if?" forever.

So *can* you be a star? Well, maybe. There's certainly nothing wrong with being a star, but that shouldn't be your motivation to embark on a career as a solo artist. There are obvious pros and cons to being a solo artist; the two biggest advantages are having complete creative control of everything and building your own brand (vs. that of a band). There are tons of additional advantages: no hassles with band contracts, band disputes, someone not showing up at practice (or a gig!), personality conflicts, and so forth. The biggest drawbacks are having no immediate support among fellow band members, and since you're a "one-man (or woman) band," you're often drawn away from music-related activities to business ones. Plus, there's naturally more work overall since the labor obviously can't be divided up among other band members. (But as Prince said, that comes with the job!)

Being a solo artist is akin to running your own business. Well, it *is* having your own business. So if you've never had experience running a business before (and even if you have), you're going to need a support system of some sort. Even if it's only one other person if you're just starting out, that person can help hold you accountable in several areas: financially, creatively, and otherwise (as long as he or she is up to the task). You'll also need incredible doses of self-discipline, self-confidence, and motivation since you won't have a boss looking over your shoulder providing you with daily goals, guidance, and a steady paycheck. But if done successfully, the potential payoff can bring tremendous rewards.

Still reading? Not scared off yet? If you've made up your mind that you definitely want to be a solo artist, then go for it! The purpose of this book is to give you the tools to help make your dreams come true (and also to encourage you to do so). Accordingly, here are several checklists to make sure you pass the litmus test of whether or not you have "the right stuff" to become a successful solo artist, along with additional checklists to strategically map out your journey to success.

DO YOU HAVE WHAT IT TAKES?

Successful artists have these common denominators among them:

1. Passion

Solo artists are so incredibly passionate and driven to succeed as artists that they will do *anything* that's legally and morally acceptable to make it happen and to sustain it when it does. They are confident and adventurous and don't see failure as an option (only as a learning experience to get to the next successful step on their journey).

2. True Talent

Of course, being talented is the foundation to becoming a successful artist. And such talent should be recognized by people other than loved ones and best friends. Many times, those closest to you will tell you (correctly or incorrectly) if they think you have talent. But people who care for you the most sometimes have their own agenda. A budding artist needs an objective opinion of his or her level of talent. Teachers, contest judges, and so on can be a great source for that sort of review. On the other hand, don't let only one of those people determine your opinion of your own talent. History is replete with the "experts" who told aspiring artists to "do something else." The artist-to-be needs a variety of objective opinions and then must glean a consensus of those opinions. (And yes, those closest to you can certainly offer their opinion as well, but remember, it's generally harder for them to be objective.)

3. Strong Work Ethic

Making a living as a solo artist is potentially the most difficult thing you'll ever do in your career. It takes a lot of work, creativity, ingenuity, connections, networking, and so forth. Be ready to educate yourself by seeking advice from those who are doing (or have done) it for a living, putting in long hours, learning from your mistakes, and so on.

4. Live Lean and within Means

Artists are passionate about their art and put "creature comforts" second (or third, fourth, or fifth) on their list. If being a working solo artist only able to afford basic necessities is acceptable to you, then you're on the right track. Substantial financial success may—or may not—come eventually in your career. But the true solo artist doesn't put big money at the top of the list (and most times, not on the list at all).

5. Patience

Career success has very rarely come overnight for big artists. And if it does come, it's often fleeting. Instead of banking on a "big break" and then becoming frustrated if it doesn't happen, the best solo artists patiently, persistently, and positively chip away at their careers one day at a time. They work on advances each day, be it obtaining a great gig at a successful local establishment or landing an interview with a local AM radio station or meeting a potential new cowriter at a local writers' roundtable. Regular benchmarks of success will add up through the months and years to the ultimate goal of sharing one's art with as many people as possible, having an impact on and/or entertaining others, and being able to make a living at it.

6. Serious Practice

Successful artists don't seek to enjoy the fruits of their labor without laboring . . . that is, practicing their craft regularly, and that means rehearsing and taking care of their "chops." Those chops may be vocal and/or instrumental (and songwriting), but in whatever way they perform, they stay in shape. And they seek to improve their craft as well. The solo artist world is unbelievably competitive, and artists need to be at the top of their game physically, mentally, and emotionally to compete effectively. Just as an Olympic athlete learns to embrace the consistent and often grueling countless hours of practice it takes to compete, so should professional artists. And if such discipline and practice isn't something you can learn to embrace as a part of the picture, perhaps you should see music as a hobby.

It's usually better to practice for a short time every day than to practice one day a week for several hours. It's much easier to build muscle memory and technique this way. If you play a classical instrument or sing, consider joining a school band, orchestra, or choir. These provide further instruction and opportunities. Playing and singing at church is also a common way of getting started. Iconic artists such as Dolly Parton and Whitney Houston got started by singing in church.

7. Resourceful

If you aren't independently wealthy, you're going to need a way to make a living while you're building your career. Solo artists find a way to stay afloat one way or another while pursuing their dreams. That may mean having a "day job" of some sort . . . or maybe a few part-time jobs to pay your rent and put food on the table while you press your spare time into service on getting paying gigs, practicing your craft, and so forth. Also, if there aren't readily available gigs (or the phone isn't ringing with offers to perform), create opportunities to share your talent: for example, local restaurants which haven't had live music before might welcome it, so reach out to some key ones and offer your services (on a limited basis) for free in locations which would offer you good exposure to get future paying gigs. In other words, don't wait for the phone to ring . . . get out there and make it happen!

GET YOUR GROOVE ON

Once you've determined and affirmed that you're truly solo artist material, then it's time to dig into the next phase of development, and that's more nuts-and-bolts research and strategizing for your career. Here's the next checklist for your journey:

1. Discover Your Best Style

Don't focus on performing a type of music that isn't completely natural to you. Clues as to what you're best at performing include the type(s) of music you like the most. Who are your musical heroes? These are clues as to where you'll be most comfortable stylistically as a performer.

2. Do Your Homework

When you've zeroed in on your best and most enjoyed type of music, research your competitors. You'll clearly be influenced by your musical heroes . . . and they had their own influences as well. But find out how your own heroes got their start. How did they succeed? Read as many articles and watch as many interviews with them as possible, read their album liner notes, and so forth. In other words, become an expert on those musical heroes of yours to see how they got to where they are, be they living or dead. Every path to success is different, but you can learn a lot about how someone made it to make his or her dreams come true.

3. Find a Coach

Most major recording artists have teachers and coaches who have helped (and continue to help) them with their craft. There are rock guitarists or pop singers who were classically trained on Mozart, Bach, and Beethoven. That's certainly not to say a classical background is necessary for your career. But the classical masters didn't become the masters for no reason. The depth and intricacy of their music have inspired pop and rock artists for decades. And if you do use a traditional teacher for your technique, you should balance out that training with additional training from a teacher or mentor who is on the contemporary side of things.

4. Expand Your Horizons

Making a living as a recording artist is difficult, as stated before, so the more parts of the music business you're versed in, the better your chances of succeeding. Don't only learn how to perform, but learn how to produce, write songs, and understand the fundamentals of music publishing. All of these areas of expertise will help you become a well-rounded professional who knows if and when you're being slickered.

5. Network

Meet as many fellow artists as possible. It doesn't matter how "big" or "small" those artists are, there is something to learn from everyone. Learn from their successes and failures and use them as your own personal learning guide. Start going to shows in your town and introducing yourself. Meet people as much as you can and tell them you're a musician. Advertise on craigslist or other local online venues to meet other musicians. Find a message board for local musicians or put up flyers in the record store or music store, old-school style, to start a performers' night or writers' roundtable at a local restaurant or bar.

GET THE SHOW ON THE ROAD!

Now that you've strategized, done your homework, and so on, it's time to put your plan into action. Here are the top 10 ways to make that happen:

1. It's Showtime

If you've never played in front of a live audience before, start small. Invite some friends and family members to watch you perform in a private setting (such as a church fellowship hall or elementary school auditorium . . . use your network of contacts to get into those places for free) and get their honest feedback and criticism. They'll most likely be gentle with their critique, and that actually can be good for your first gig. That can set the stage for your next performance, which could be a local restaurant or club that is public yet relatively small and manageable. Lots of coffee shops and bars will offer open mic nights, which are designed to give first-timers a crack at the stage. Almost everyone at an open mic will be inexperienced, so it's an easy and understanding audience.

2. Lay It Down

If you want to be a recording artist, then record! You have to start somewhere, because that's ultimately how you'll learn and improve in the recording process. You can start with some acoustic songs on the built-in mic on your cell phone. Then, check out Ableton, GarageBand, FL Studio (formerly FruityLoops), and other types of inexpensive software that are wonderfully user-friendly tools to help you get started. More advanced (and expensive) recording software include ProTools and Logic. These programs will help you graduate to a more professional sound. You'll be amazed at how professional you can sound with these programs.

3. *Three's a Crowd*

After you've experimented and learned by doing it yourself for your initial recordings and if no record labels are knocking at your door just yet, you'll want to consider hiring a professional engineer and booking studio time to make your first EP (extended-play recording). An EP is shorter than an album but more than one song, usually about four to six cuts, and used primarily for promotional purposes (hopefully as a tool to land a record deal). If you don't have a lot of money lying around just waiting to be spent, you can seek crowd funding. Platforms such as Kickstarter, GoFundMe, and Indiegogo are all excellent tools to seek funding for your first EP. Be ready to offer those who participate some sort of premium in exchange for their support (obviously offer a copy of the EP to all who send in some money). Be sure to read the rules of engagement on each site carefully so as to make sure you're legally and completely following their protocol.

4. *Hit the Web*

Use the Internet and all its tools to your advantage. Besides having your own domain name and website where you promote releases and shows, you'll probably want a presence on the main social media sites, such as Facebook, Twitter, and Instagram. Start separate social networking pages for yourself as an artist. Invite all of your own followers to follow that page for updates about gigs, new recordings, and other information about your music career. Bandcamp, SoundCloud, DatPiff, and BAND are all excellent tools that allow you to share high-quality sound files of your music and follow other bands, labels, and accounts for free. But don't overcommit your time. If you spend all day working on social media, what happens to your music? It's better to skip some social media rather than do a poor or infrequent job of staying in touch with your fan base. And of course, you'll want to make access to your music easy through YouTube, SoundCloud, the iTunes Store, CD Baby, and the like. Last, but definitely not least, build and use an email list to stay connected with your fans. Permission-based marketing (such as MailChimp) by sending emails to your fan base is a proven winner—these are folks who said they wanted to stay in touch!

Many beginning artists eventually secure lucrative record deals because of their beginnings on YouTube. These artists found a way to do either audio–only or video–plus–audio versions of their songs (more on video next). If your YouTube performance goes viral (or at least gets a huge number of viewings), that will be something you can tout to a record label when you're shopping your recording to them. (See "In the Mix" in this chapter for further details about contract negotiation.)

5. Lights, Camera, Action!

Whether you're in a band or a solo artist, making a video of you per-forming your music is a must. But walk before you run! Make sure you've focused completely on creating great songs and have gleaned enough ex-perience through live performances before you step in front of the camera. And at first, the camera can be on your cell phone. There are plenty of inexpensive editing programs available plus unlimited "how-to" free on-line videos and books to teach yourself how to make professional-looking videos. But make sure you're ready for a video before you spend the time (or any money) cooking one up.

6. Work Up to a Tour

As you rehearse, record, and share your music online, it's important to connect with fans in a live setting as well—for most styles of music. Try to grow your fan base by playing regular gigs and organizing a tour when it's financially possible. Keep it local at first. Find a few local venues where you'll be able to play regular shows and try to get in tight with the management. Be reliable, consistent, and professional, and bring a crowd. They'll ask you back. Try to book a short tour when you're first starting out. World tours with shows in Iceland and Japan probably aren't feasible for your first tours. Keep it to the tristate area, no more than a week or two at most. Tour fund-ing ideas include donations from family and friends; crowdfunding websites (Kickstarter, PledgeMusic, Sellaband, FeedBands, etc.); getting a part-time job; revenue from e-commerce sales on your website; and setting aside a por-tion of money from regular gigs earmarked for touring expenses.

7. Bring on the Merch!

A cool looking T-shirt with your name and logo on it, a few trendy patches, and other music-related merchandise is like free advertising for your music career. Every time someone wears the T-shirt with your name, logo, and/or image on it there's the possibility that a few more people might get interested and check you out. Merchandise is also an excellent way to make money and sustain your cash flow or to make a little money for recording and other costs associated with a solo career. If you've got cool-looking stuff to sell, you can make quite a bit of money at a single gig between merch, ticket sales, and guaranteed fees from the venue.

8. Grow to a Larger Market

If you live in a small town, it's going to be tough to get noticed by a wider fan base, regardless of the kind of music you play. Shows at the coffee shop around the corner are a great start. But think about whether it would benefit your music career to move to a bigger city where there will be more opportunities. New York and Los Angeles are definitely places to get noticed, although it can be hard to crack into such a big scene. Consider moving to a more local big city first. Chicago or Minneapolis are good bets in the Midwest. Providence or Philadelphia are music towns on the East Coast. Nashville or Austin represent the South, and Portland or Seattle hold it down on the West Coast.

Play gigs outside of the usual clubs that cater to your genre of music. Branch out a bit, consider gigs at schools, fairs, festivals, and perhaps parks in the summertime. So many artists think that the only valid venues to play are clubs. Look around, start noticing where you see performers playing music, and ask yourself if that venue isn't a valid one for you. Give your fans more than one place to see you perform while finding new followers. And at every gig, be sure there is an email sign-up sheet.

9. Get Real

Try out for a reality show. Yes, a reality show! One excellent short-cut to exposure is to get yourself on television. Even if you don't win, an appearance can be huge exposure. This can give you important industry contacts. Find those 15 minutes of fame and use them to further your ambitions. Talent-based performance shows like *American Idol, The X Factor, The Voice,* and others will often be a good way to get exposure to a mainstream audience as a potential recording artist. It's a good way to see if you have what it takes. MTV and other music programs will sometimes host shows searching for the "next big star" of some particular style.

10. Be Consistent

Make sure the message you communicate is consistent . . . musically, graphically, color-wise, sound-wise, design-wise, and so forth. Don't send mixed messages. As with any successful ad campaign, make sure your brand is consistent and presents a unified message. See building your brand as being akin to an integrated ad campaign.

READY FOR THE BIG TIME

As you have built your career steadily through practice, hard work, and all of the above, you could be ready and primed to grab the golden ticket: getting a record deal. Nowadays, some independent artists aren't interested in record deals . . . they feel the complete creative freedom they have without a deal is more attractive. And there's a lot of truth in that. However, most artists—even now with the overall diminished power of the traditional record label model—still want a record deal. It remains the fastest path to mass exposure for you and your art. Record contracts often include guarantees and advances, which don't require you to sell a lot. If you've got a single you know will sell a million copies, you stand to make a lot of money from iTunes alone, but if you're not sure you can deliver, a recording contract offers you more security.

There are good record deals and bad ones. There are small, medium, and large labels. Your job is to do your homework (once again) as to which are the good and bad deals and labels so that you can make an informed decision. This book is designed to help you understand the fundamentals of the entire music business, therefore providing you with the tools to discern the good labels from the bad ones. And don't sign the first label deal that comes along without doing a great deal of research on that label.

Here's the next checklist on the steps to getting a recording deal:

1. Record a Professional Demo

If you want to get signed to a label, you need to have a high-quality demo recording of your music to share. Normally, the best way to do this is online, so it's helpful to update those old Bandcamp and SoundCloud accounts to represent your best-sounding recordings of your highest-quality material. Most good demos are no more than a song or two. Record your hits, your absolute best material. No filler. Remember: Labels don't sign artists because they hope they'll record great music one day. They sign talent who already records great music, then they provide that artist with a push from which they hope to profit.

2. Prepare a Press Package

Press packages are used to accompany demo tapes. The press package should explain who you are, what you do, and where you come from in a concise way. A basic press package should involve the following items:

- A short bio explaining who you are
- Photos
- Newspaper and/or Internet write-ups
- Interviews
- Reviews
- Quotes or endorsements from other artists

3. Think about Your Image

The quality of your music is the most important part of a career in the music industry. But talent won't take you all the way. To be successful, having a look that matches your sound is usually an important consideration in marketing yourself as an artist. Use your sound to influence your look and vice versa. If you look like a burly woodsman, it might be a good idea to emphasize the gruffer, more folk-like elements of your sound. If you're a clean-cut city dweller, on the other hand, it might be a good idea to get some dirt under your fingernails and grow a beard if you want to be in a successful bluegrass band.

4. Send Your Material to Labels That Support Your Style of Music

Who put out your favorite artists' records? Where did they get their start? Who do you know at particular labels who might be willing to give you a shot at a recording? Pick a few labels you think you might have a chance with and send their A&R (artists and repertoire . . . more on that in a later chapter) department your demo and press package. Major labels like Warner Bros., Virgin, and Sony BMG have a lot of money to throw around at established acts, but they typically only look at groups that have big potential to make money. Many of the acts will have multiple albums or industry success under their belts already. Independent labels might have less money, but they are more willing to give you control over your product. There's typically more freedom with an "indie" label. Some people think the more labels you send you material out to, the better chance you'll have of getting signed. It's important to be familiar with the labels you're contacting. Never engage in a "carpet-bombing" campaign. If you're sending your demo of folk tunes to metal labels, you're wasting everyone's time.

5. Play a Label Showcase

An alternative way of getting noticed and potentially signed by a record label is to try to find out about industry showcases and festivals or travel to one for a gig. You can typically apply to showcases by submitting materials and then play and network when you're there. For many acts, this is the best way to get actual face time with talent scouts. South by Southwest (SXSW) in Austin, Texas, is one of the best places for upstart DIY acts to get noticed by the music industry, but any type of music festival is huge exposure for a band. Even if the stage you play on is the smallest one, it's great to be able to say that your name was on the bill with other big acts.

YOUR SURVIVAL KIT

Being a solo artist is challenging, and not just on a creative level—according to researchers, working as a solo artist can actually be hazardous to your health(!). A recent study of almost 1,500 career musicians found that over 50 years, solo artists were twice as likely to die than artists who were members of bands! While it's not clear exactly why solo performers have a shorter life expectancy than that of other musicians, anyone who has worked as a solo artist will tell you that they face a host of extra pressures that bands don't have to deal with. Perhaps it's time for solo performers to put some serious thought into preserving their mental health, and with that in mind, here are a few strategies to consider:

1. Mix It Up

Many of the problems that solo artists deal with stem from one main issue: isolation. It can be very easy to get stuck in your own little bubble both creatively and emotionally when you're a one-person act. The best way to get out of that bubble is simply to work with other musicians, even if it's just the occasional jam. Even though technology has allowed us to create and consume music in isolation, music is fundamentally a communal phenomenon, and it's important to keep that communal feeling alive, even if you create music on your own most of the time.

2. You Need You

When a solo performer says they need time off to look after themselves, it may sound like their ego is getting out of control, but logic indicates that solo artists really do need more time for self-care. If you're in a band and you play a bad show or release an album that flops, there's some consolation in the fact that what you did was a group effort. But as a solo artist, the success or failure of a project reflects 100 percent on you, even if you had other people involved in the creation of your work. That's why it's important to take time off when you need to—since there's more pressure on you, it's natural for you to need more time to deal with that pressure.

3. Put on a Persona

Whether you perform under your own name or under an alias, separating your professional life from your personal life can be a real challenge as a solo artist. When you play in a band, the band often becomes its own entity, separate from your personality and the personalities of your bandmates, but when you are the band, you and your personality become the entity. And while sometimes it can be helpful to your artistic pursuits to showcase your true personality when performing publicly, there's also something to be said for keeping some parts of your life to yourself. That's why many solo artists (e.g., Lady Gaga, David Bowie, Bob Dylan) inhabit a persona (or even several different personas) when they perform. A persona allows you to market yourself more clearly to your audience, and at the same time it can be another method you use to deal with the pressure of being a solo performer.

4. Protect Your Assets

While a developing a persona can help you separate the personal from the professional in the psychological sense, it's also important to think about separating these two elements financially. Artists are well known for funding their passion projects out of their own pockets, and when your passion project has your name attached to it, the line between your personal finances and your music career finances can become dangerously thin.

That's why it's important for solo artists to protect their assets through smart financial management. Depending on where you are in your career, it may or may not be beneficial to form something like an LLC (limited liability corporation) to manage your finances, but at the very least, it's a good idea to keep separate bank accounts for personal and business use. An LLC is a legal form of a company that provides limited liability to its owners in many jurisdictions. LLCs are well known for the flexibility that they provide to business owners; depending on the situation, an LLC may elect to use corporate tax rules instead of being treated as a partnership, and under certain circumstances, LLCs may be organized as not for profit. Any accountant and/or tax attorney can give full details about the ultimate benefits of an LLC, plus the tax credits that can come with it.

5. Help! You Need Somebody!

In today's music business, there are plenty of ways to build a career without being signed to a record label. But just because it's possible to do everything on your own doesn't mean it's necessarily a good idea. While bands are able to divide up tasks like booking tours, posting on social media, bookkeeping, and everything else that goes along with being an artist, solo performers are largely on their own in this respect. On the flip side, solo artists don't have to split their earnings with bandmates, which leaves more money in the pot to hire people like publicists, managers, and booking agents to take some of the workload off of their shoulders.

To the average listener, there isn't much difference between a solo artist and a band—we listen to music because we want to feel something, and it doesn't really matter whether that feeling comes from a single person or a group of 10 people. Which is to say that while we may not be doing it on purpose, the way we listen to music actually puts a good deal more pressure on solo acts than it does on bands. If you're a solo artist, take a moment to congratulate yourself on how difficult your job is. Then get back out there and make some more music—just don't be afraid to ask for some help along the way.

NOW FOR THE *DON'TS*

Thus far in this chapter, we've discussed what to do to become a successful solo artist. Here is a final checklist of the things to avoid on your journey:

1. Take Nothing for Granted

Realize that no one is waiting for your music. If people are going to become fans of your music, you must approach the promoting of your live shows and the promotion of your CD releases with the same planning and professionalism as the artists whom you admire have promoted their music. Marketing music has changed radically in the age of the Internet and social media. That technology has the potential to take your music to the world. But knowing that it is up to *you* to let the world know about your music is an important first step to take as a responsible independent musician.

2. Don't Do "Good"

Avoid telling people in the music business that your music is "good." It is a much overused and weak word. A&R reps, music directors at radio stations, the music press, and buyers at distributors and stores presume you think your music is "good" because you put it out to begin with. When they listen to it, they will decide if it is the kind of "good" music that they feel they can get behind and be proud of supporting from their position of power in the music industry. And let's face it, it is the public who will ultimately decide if your music is "good" by buying it or not. That's not to say you shouldn't talk up your music. But use your words; shape an elevator pitch that accurately reflects what you and your music are about.

3. Don't Forget "the Little People"

Thank people who help you. You might be surprised how often music reviewers, DJs at college radio stations, and club bookers don't get thanked by artists. So make their day by sending a card, a small thank-you gift, or simply by giving them a shout-out on the tray card of your next CD. Some artists tend to feel they are owed something because of their talent. Guess what . . . they aren't. Being grateful and thankful are essential qualities for success. Cultivate them and watch the doors open.

4. Stay Fresh!

Listen to other kinds of music beyond your own particular genre. There is much to be learned from other styles. All music offers a vast reservoir of new melodies and rhythms to experiment with and to incorporate into your unique sound. If the future of music promises anything, it is the ongoing mix of old and new styles coming together in profoundly new ways.

5. Don't Conform

Remember that the record labels sometimes don't know what they are looking for, but with any luck, they will recognize it when they hear it. Work on developing your own signature sound rather than trying to shape something to please A&R people or future fans. Strive to find your own true identity through your music. And don't feel like once you've established a musical identity it needs to be set in stone. Great artists such as Bob Dylan and Neil Young have continually reinvented their personas and music throughout their careers.

6. Don't Be a Graphic Geek

How many logos do you have in your brain right now that are recognizable symbols for legendary bands? You want to build the same kind of "brand awareness" for your music by creating a memorable logo and graphics. Make sure the logo is legible/identifiable in a wide range of sizes and that you use it everywhere your name appears: on posters, flyers, press releases, letters, business cards, stationery, websites, and CD covers.

7. Don't Repeat Your Mistakes

As the old saying goes, insanity has been described as repeating the same habit continually while expecting a different result. As a musician, you may find yourself not wanting to rehearse yet frustrated that your musical abilities never progress. Or as a songwriter, you may get upset when you keep backing yourself into a corner with an awkward rhyme scheme yet find yourself continuing to use it. All artists at times get trapped in creative dead ends, but the way out is not through repeating the same moves that got us there in the first place. Challenge yourself to find new inspirations and develop at least one new creative technique a month.

8. Don't Stop the Music!

One sure way to gain some level of success as a musician is simply to continue being one. There is no one timetable or path to success. Most artists termed *overnight successes* are in reality years in the making. If you find yourself approaching the creative act of making music as a chore, what is the point in that? Some of the most successful musicians out there are people who simply never stopped making their own music, performing it regularly, and finding a comfortable way to go about doing the business of their music. They could never *not* make music. Are you that passionate? Would a part of you die without your being able to make your music? If so, just keep doing it, the rest will follow. The music industry has always been competitive and cutthroat at heart, and these days income is becoming harder and harder to find. Making a little money playing music on the side isn't so hard, but in order to turn a passion into a career, you have to want it more than anything else. Though there is a ton of luck involved, many factors can be influenced to put you in a position to launch a musical career. However, it's important not to have unrealistic standards about how things will be once you're able to quit your "day job."

In the Mix: Contract Negotiation

Contract negotiation can be intimidating and unnerving, especially for beginning artists. A lot can be at stake, but if the artist is prepared with some basic contract-negotiation fundamentals, the process can go smoother and more successfully. Here are a few simple tips to keep in mind.

1. *Seek "win/win" negotiations.* As cliché as it may sound, when you are truly interested in both parties getting what—or as much as possible—each wants, you are then engaged in win/win negotiating. Try to see the negotiation as a way to help each side of the table achieve mutually beneficial goals and a dynamic that is positive and will foster getting to an agreeable outcome. Read *Getting to Yes: Negotiating Agreement without Giving In* by Roger Fisher, Bruce Patton, and William Ury, a classic book regarding positive negotiations.
2. *Be reasonable.* Beginning artists sometimes make the mistake of getting an overly aggressive attorney to negotiate a deal. Attorneys who aren't familiar with the music business (and therefore what is and isn't the norm for beginning artists in terms of royalty rates, etc.) often ask for too much on behalf of their client, thus scaring the potential record label away. If a record label "sniffs" that a potential

new artist is going to be high maintenance, they sometimes get cold feet and back out of doing a deal. Do your homework and find a reputable attorney who has done the sort of deal you're considering and move ahead accordingly. The book *Bargaining for Advantage: Negotiation Strategies for Reasonable People* by G. Richard Shell is an excellent resource along these lines.

3. *Be sympathetic.* Each person on either side of the negotiation table potentially has something to gain and to lose. Realize that the person with whom you're negotiating also has fears during a negotiation, so be sympathetic and remember to put yourself in his or her shoes as you seek to come to a mutually beneficial outcome.

4. *Know what you want.* Have a clear picture of exactly what it is you want out of the negotiation. Know what your "deal breakers" are and are not.

5. *Don't be afraid to walk away.* Sometimes when a truly win/win agreement cannot be reached, don't be afraid to walk away. And if you choose to walk away because a mutually beneficial agreement

6

FROM SONG TO SELLING

Music Publishing

For beginners or the uninitiated, the music business can seem like a glamorous profession . . . especially if one has his or her sights set on being a recording artist or songwriter. The idea of music publishing can seem dowdy or boring in the face of performing hit songs, walking the red carpet on Grammy night, or attending a champagne party for a hit song. But the truth is . . . "sexy" or not . . . music publishing lies at the heart of the music business. As has been stated before in this book, "It all begins with a song," but without music publishers, no one ever hears the song. Or sees it (as in the case of printed music).

Music publishing can be a daunting subject and task for the uninitiated (or even for the initiated, for that matter). In other words, don't try this at home! (Or should you? See "In the Mix" in this chapter.)

Music publishing is complex in many ways. As with many areas of the music business, art and commerce collide head-on in this crucial area of the music industry. Add to that the legal considerations, as well as with distribution (be it physical or digital), and things get complex fast. Yet by the same token, music publishing is very simple, for at its center lies the basic desire of a publisher to share great music with as wide an audience as possible (i.e., to change the world positively with the transforming power of music!). By exploiting a composer's song (*exploiting* is a good word in this context), the publisher then ensures the composer will be remunerated fairly through the multitude of potential revenue streams where the song can be used in order for the composer (and publisher) to maintain a livelihood (i.e., *eat!*).

Simply put, the function of music publishing is to serve as a conduit to get the music from the creator(s) to the public.

Music creator→ Publisher → Public

With the advent and explosion of the Internet, digital publishing, social media platforms, and other methods to introduce one's songs to the world, some question the need nowadays for a traditional music publisher. But most composers—after trying to to it themselves—soon realize it's better to let the publisher be the publisher so they can focus on writing. So the publisher's role is key to the songwriter. And as discussed in chapter 3, whoever owns the copyright holds the key to the revenue streams, and the publisher owns the copyright, which occurs only after the composer (and lyricist, if applicable) has *assigned* the copyright to the publisher. This is accomplished by the writer(s) signing a contract prepared by the publisher. Without this assignment of copyright to the publisher, the original copyright continues to rest with the creator(s) of the song.

The body of copyrights contained in the music publisher's repertoire is called a *catalog*, and some music catalogs generate millions—even billions—of dollars each year.

INSIDE A MUSIC PUBLISHER

Most people have never been inside a music publisher, so what ultimately goes on inside one can be a mystery of sorts. The largest music publishers (such as Sony/ATV, Universal Music, and Warner/Chappell) contain numerous departments: creative, promotional, business/legal affairs, licensing, finance, copyright, royalties, IT (information techology), plus the executive management team (president/CEO, COO, CFO, vice president(s), and other upper managers). However, the vast number of music publishers in the world are much smaller operations, sometimes with as few as one or two people (sometimes referred to as a "vest pocket" music publisher).

A BRIEF HISTORY OF MUSIC PUBLISHING

The word *publishing* has verb and noun forms. "I am going to *publish* your song" (verb) or "I'm a *publisher*" (noun). Or if a songwriter says, "I want to keep the *publishing* of my song" that means they want to retain ownership of their song. So in that sense, the word *publishing* is a noun. (But *publishing* generally equals *ownership* of the copyright of the song, regardless of how the word is used in a sentence. An exception to a publisher owning the copyright is in the case of print publishers, who may not actually own the copyright of a song but have licensed it. For example, print publishers who are in the pop music business—for example, Alfred Music and Hal Leonard Corporation—seldom own the pop copyrights they are publishing in printed form. More on print publishers later in this chapter.)

In the early days of music publishing, when someone said "I am going to publish your song" it meant "I am going to release your song as sheet music." Print music publishers are still alive and well, and in their case publishing one's song does indeed mean putting it into sheet music. But at the beginning of modern music publishing, it *always* meant printing the song in sheet music form. Indeed, many of the earliest music publishers also owned printing presses. The early years of successful, commercial music publishing in the United States centered around Tin Pan Alley. This was the name given to the collection of New York City music publishers and songwriters located on a strip of row houses at West 28th Street between Fifth and Sixth Avenues in Manhattan. These publishers dominated the popular music of the United States in the late 19th and early 20th century (see figure 6.1). It can be said without exaggeration that these blocks are where the American popular music industry began and saw its most prolific and diverse output. The name Tin Pan Alley is sometimes still used as a figurative term for the entire U.S. music business.

Tin Pan Alley traces its beginnings back to around 1885, when a plethora of music publishers opened in that small section of New York City. When Tin Pan Alley's heyday actually ended isn't as clear, but it's generally regarded to have declined at the start of the Great Depression when the then new technologies of phonograph players, radio, and motion pictures replaced sheet music as the dominant delivery system of music into the home. Others claim Tin Pan Alley's influence lasted into the early 1950s when rock and roll came into the picture.[1] The Brill Building (located on Broadway in New York City) became a hub of such rock-and-roll songwriting activity (documented expertly in the hit Broadway musical *Beautiful: The Carole King Musical*).

In those days, *song pluggers* were pianists who played songs to get them heard. The song pluggers (sometimes called *song demonstrators* if working in a department store) were pianists who were hired by music publishers of the day to help them promote and sell new sheet music of their songs.[2] Legendary composers George Gershwin and Jerome Kern originally worked as song pluggers before they became famous.

As legend has it, in the days before air-conditioning was invented, the music publishers that populated Tin Pan Alley would raise their windows in the summer. Their song pluggers were plunking away on pianos, pitching tunes, and if one walked through the alley hearing the blended cacophony

Fig 6.1. Tin Pan Alley

of the percussive playing of cheap, upright pianos, it was said to sound like someone was banging tin pans together. Hence, the name Tin Pan Alley caught on.

The exploitation of songs by music publishers soon graduated to a much wider method with the invention of phonographs, then radio, television, and so on, making Tin Pan Alley a distant memory. In the face of these new, growing revenue streams, print music became less attractive to music publishers of the day since printed music was (and is) so labor intensive. To produce printed music required music engraving (called as such because in its earliest form of production, music note heads were on hammers that were struck into copper plates—or engraved—and then the copper plates were inked and used to print sheet music. See figure 6.2). Before the music was engraved and printed, it had to be edited. Plus, to experience sheet music performed required someone who could sing and play piano or another instrument. The process of professionally putting notes on paper for publication is still called *engraving* today, but the copper-plate procedure evolved into a series of other technologies and eventually into modern, sophisticated computer-software programs.

When the phonograph was invented, to hear music all one had to do was put on a record, crank the phonograph, and *voilà . . .* music! The process was even easier when radio came along. Turn a knob and there could be a full orchestral concert coming into one's living room. No longer was published, printed sheet music necessary to have music in one's home. Accordingly,

Fig 6.2.   Early Music Engraving

sheet music sales declined rapidly, and music publishers of the day farmed out their print music rights to companies that specialized in printed music. As the digital age has continued to creep into music publishing, there's been a consolidation of print music publishers. And while there are still dozens and dozens of independent print music publishers remaining in the world (secular and sacred), there are really only two major print publishers remaining: Hal Leonard Corporation and Alfred Music.

With the advent of the aforementioned then new revenue streams, and as music publishers relied much less on printed music as a form of the distribution of their songs, revenues grew. And those revenues always came back to the music publisher . . . the song owner. And the publisher, in turn, paid royalties to the composers. Therefore, as stated as the beginning of this chapter, although music publishing might seemingly lack the "sizzle" of the record or songwriting business, since the music business revolves around songs, all "roads" (i.e., revenue streams) lead back to the music publisher. Record companies, television, radio, and film producers (and the list can go on) all pay music publishers to use songs in their respective venues. And to procure those songs requires *licenses* granted from the music publisher.

TYPES OF PUBLISHING LICENSES

There are two major types of licenses that music publishers issue to people, companies, and organizations who want to use their songs: mechanical and synchronization licenses. Another significant license is a print license for those companies wishing to use a copyrighted song in music print format.

A *mechanical license* grants the rights to "reproduce and distribute copyrighted musical compositions (songs) on CDs, records, tapes, ringtones, permanent digital downloads, interactive streams and other digital configurations supporting various business models, including locker-based music services and bundled music offerings."[3]

Most music publishers in the United States choose to have their mechanical rights administered by the Harry Fox Agency (HFA). Established in 1927 by the National Music Publishers Association (NMPA), HFA is the number-one provider of rights management, licensing, and royalty services in the U.S. music industry. They are primarily known for collecting and distributing mechanical royalties on behalf of music publishers.[4]

A *synchronization license* (or "synch" for short) is a music license granted by a copyright holder for use of a song in visual media (e.g., video, television, video games.).[5]

When it comes to the protection of a song, a copyright embodies two components: the song itself and the recording of that song (if, indeed, there is a recording made of the song, and of course, there's usually always a recording made). In chapter 3, we discussed the "bundle of rights" to which a copyright owner is entitled. But what about the company, person, or entity that owns the sound recording? Well, that entity (most often a record label) also has a copyright for the master recording—separate from the song copyright.[6] This ownership of the *master recording* is not designated with a © but a ℗. This stands for *phonorecord*.

When someone desires to publish a song in print (or digital print) format, a *print license* must be obtained from the copyright owner. The terms are usually that the copyright owner be paid a 12.5 percent royalty (of suggested retail price) for each copy of sheet music sold. Digital rates are higher, generally 50 percent of suggested retail price for each copy of music downloaded.

MUSIC PUBLISHING PRIMARY REVENUE STREAMS

In addition to mechanical (CD and record sales—both physical and digital versions) and synch licensing revenues, music publishers have a variety of other ways to exploit songs and generate money.

1. Public Performances

When a song is performed publicly, the creator and publisher of that song are entitled to be remunerated for its use. For example, when a restaurant plays recorded music (or has "live" music performed), the purpose of that music is to add value to the dining experience. Some restaurant owners originally argued that they had purchased the CD or radio or piano from which the music was coming and therefore they should not be required to pay additional money for the use of that music. But the copyright law delineates the public performance of music as a separate and equal right entitled to the copyright owner, and it is remunerated separately. Besides, if the public performance of music had no value (in this case, to enhance the dining experience), it wouldn't be used. But music *does* enhance our daily lives and experiences and is so often present that we don't even realize it. Malls, theme parks, sporting events, elevators, hotel lobbies, movie theaters, skating rinks, health clubs . . . and on the list can go. These are all places where music is played or performed publicly ("live" or recorded) as a means to *enhance the experience.* Therefore, music has value in these venues, and its creators and publishers are entitled to be remunerated accordingly. For the average person who isn't in the business of making music for a living, it's sometimes hard to understand this, since the long-held, popular way of thinking is often "music should be free . . . like the air we breathe." With the explosion of online "sharing" of music files (a polite word for stealing), music has been devalued all the more and it is harder than ever to make a case for its inherent worth. Still, the law is the law, and the law exists in order to preserve the livelihood of music creators and publishers and ensure the creation of quality new music now and in the future.

Broadcast (television, radio) or cable/satellite use of songs also constitutes a public performance of music, even when the performance isn't "live." This form of performance comprises the largest revenue portion of public performance revenues for the music publisher/songwriter.

As it regards remuneration for the public performance of music, however, it is important to note that certain nonprofit organizations, such as churches, are exempt from having to pay for the public performance of music, although law-abiding churches belong to CCLI (Christian Copyright Licensing International) to legally cover their reproduction of lyric/music-screen projections or in the printed program, music recorded for shut-ins, praise band use, and so forth. To learn more about CCLI, visit www.ccli.com.

The four performing rights organizations (PROs) that, in essence, serve as collection agencies of public-performance income on behalf of their affiliated music publishers and songwriters are ASCAP (American Society of Composers, Authors and Publishers), BMI (Broadcast Music, Inc.), SESAC, and GMR (Global Music Rights).

Songwriters/lyricists choose to belong to one of these organizations (writers can't belong to more than one). Once a publisher publishes a song by a given writer, the publisher registers that song with the respective PRO to which the writer belongs (publishers belong to whichever PROs are necessary to accommodate their writers). Once that song appears in the PRO's survey of public performances, the PRO pays 50 percent of the revenue to the publisher and 50 percent of the revenue to the songwriter. PROs are the only organizations that pay songwriting royalties *directly* to the songwriter in addition to the publisher (music publishers receive the *entire* revenues from other sources discussed in this chapter, then remit the 50 percent "writer's share" to the songwriter and retain their 50 percent "publisher's share"). The four PROs have slightly different means and methods of surveying public performances of the music from their respective repertoires. To learn more about these survey methods, visit each PRO's website.

It is important to note that many novices in the music business often confuse PROs for music publishers. *PROs are* not *music publishers. They are not in the business of acquiring copyrights.* They are, as said before, collection agencies of public-performance income on behalf of music publishers and songwriters.

2. Motion Pictures

These song uses require a synch license (mentioned earlier), and the types of uses within films are varied: title sequence, featured performance, background, trailer, ending credits, and so on. The rate charged by the music publisher to the film's producer varies based on the type and frequency of use in the film, popularity of the song, and so forth.

3. Broadcast/Cable/Subscription

Television (local and network), cable, and subscription services (HBO, Showtime, Netflix, etc.) are all potentially lucrative revenue streams for music. These uses also require a synch license obtained by the producer from the music publisher. As with motion pictures, the rate charged by the publisher is based on the type and frequency of use, popularity of the song, and so on.

4. Commercials

When pairing the selling of a product with a familiar (or even unfamiliar song), it's a powerful combination. Music publishers are careful, however, when granting permission for producers to use a well-known song since if the advertising campaign becomes very successful, the song used can become interminably linked with a product. For example, if a standard song becomes associated with a beer, soft drink, or ketchup, it's difficult for the listener of that song (when hearing it performed "live" or otherwise) not to think of the product instead of the song. Of course, advertisers love when that happens, but a songwriter or publisher doesn't want their hit song permanently "typecast" with a particular brand of product. It's a double-edged sword since a successful ad campaign using a particular song will generate a lot of revenue for both the songwriter and publisher, but it can also "contaminate" the song's future use outside of a commercial.

Commercial jingles, on the other hand, which are written specifically for a product, can linger in the ears of the public for decades in a good way, boosting a songwriter's career (and public awareness of a product). For example, Coca-Cola's legendary "I'd Like to Teach the World to Sing" jingle (Roger Cook/Roger Greenaway).

5. Print

Believe it or not, in the digital age physical print music is still a very viable source of revenue for music publishers and their songwriters. Songbooks (often called *folios*) for piano, voice, guitar, and a full line of instruments are available in abundance for home and educational/institutional use. The educational print music market (music for schools, churches, and home use) remains viable. Apart from physical print, the digital print market continues to grow. As mentioned before, a print license is required for such song uses.

There are numerous *secondary revenue streams* for music publishers: video games, lyric reprints, greeting cards, dolls and toys, tour merchandise, ringtones, theatre (Broadway, Off-Broadway, etc.), and more. The music publisher's job is to find as many uses as possible for its catalog of songs, therefore increasing the songs' value and income to their songwriters.

PUBLISHING CONTRACTS

While there are a multitude of types of music publishing contracts, you can most always expect the following, basic elements in all of them (with the exception of a work for hire agreement where there is no transfer of copyright):

1. *Transfer of copyright.* This is the most important thing for a music publisher in the contract, and that's the transfer of ownership of the copyright from the writer to the publisher.
2. *Royalty percentage/rate.* What percentage of the revenues will you receive? As stated earlier, the standard writer's share is 50 percent. In the case of printed music, the standard rate is 10 percent of retail price of the piece of sheet music.
3. *Term.* If a songwriter signs an exclusive contract (see below), the standard length is three to five years, with one-year automatic renewals unless canceled by either party.

4. *Territory.* Where will the song be sold and promoted? Publishers always prefer to sell throughout the entire world.

Here are the most common types of song contracts:

1. Single Song Agreement

This is the simplest and most basic form of agreement in the music publishing business when a publisher is signing one song.

2. Exclusive Songwriting Contract

In this contract, the songwriter agrees to write songs only for the music publisher to which they've signed. Often an *advance royalty* is offered (royalty money paid up front in advance of actual sales taking place, which most times must be recouped before an additional advance is paid) with an exclusive agreement as one of the perks in exchange for the songwriter's exclusivity. These type of agreements rarely happen with beginning songwriters since there's no track record upon which to base the advance royalty. The advantages of such a contract for the writer include a steady paycheck and not having to "pound the pavement" pitching his or her songs to various publishers, as well as receiving prime writing assignments over nonexclusive writers. The drawbacks include a publisher possibly not delivering on its promises to fully promote the writer's songs effectively or taking the writer's talents for granted and therefore not cultivating the writer completely. But if publisher and writer know each other well before signing such an agreement, there should be no surprises before the deal is consummated (somewhat like a marriage!).

Occasionally, instead of an advance royalty, there is an agreement guaranteeing that the publisher will publish a minimum number of songs from the signed writer. In some deals, if the writer meets that minimum song amount in a given year, he or she is free to send songs to other publishers (but often with a maximum number of songs—or a "cap"—that can be sent elsewhere).

3. Copublishing Agreement

Often, exclusive writers at different companies will cowrite songs together. The resulting agreement is a copublishing agreement, where generally the ownership of the song is split 50/50 between the participating publishers. Another form of copublishing is when a writer, for various reasons, insists on retaining part ownership of the song he or she has written and places that ownership percentage with his or her own publishing company while the other participating publisher of the song retains the other portion of the copyright.

4. Work for Hire Agreement

When a songwriter is engaged by a publisher or other organization to write music or lyrics and is to receive a one-time fee or lump sum for his or her work instead of a royalty payment, this type agreement is a work for hire arrangement. One might ask why any writer would forego a potentially lucrative ongoing royalty stream in favor of a one-time fee. The answer is usually getting money immediately instead of having to wait for royalties to be paid (which are generally paid by publishers quarterly, semiannually, or annually). If a writer is hungry and needs the money now, an immediate lump sum is more attractive to help pay the mortgage versus a royalty that the songwriter won't see for about a year after the song is written by the time the song has been released, sold, and sales accounted for. Plus, if the song is a flop and doesn't sell, no royalties would have been garnered by the songwriter (and the obvious flip side of that is if the song is a hit, the up-front money received by the songwriter won't begin to come close to matching the royalty that could have eventually been received through royalty payments).

5. Administration Agreement

Larger or medium-sized publishers often do administration-only deals (or "admin" deals) with other publishers. In this scenario, the administrating publisher takes care of various publishing functions on behalf of the administrated publisher. These functions often include (though are not limited to) granting permissions for song registration, song use, payment of royalties, and even copyright exploitation. These services are often referred to as the "back office" functions of a music publisher. These back-office functions do not include song procurement, since that is the lifeblood of a music publisher and is done by the administered publisher. An admin agreement is particularly attractive to small publishers who don't have large staffs to cover these important back-office functions. The administrating publisher retains a percentage of the revenues collected on behalf of the administered publisher as its remuneration for providing these services.

6. Subpublishing Agreement

This is basically a music publishing deal in foreign territories between a U.S. publisher and a publisher in a foreign territory. They are like admin deals (with no ownership of the copyrights being transferred to the subpublisher) but generally are limited to one or more countries or regions outside the United States. Under this publishing deal, the publisher allows the subpublisher to act on its behalf in certain foreign territories. Often they are limited to a group of countries, such as the European Union (EU), GAS (Germany, Austria, Switzerland), Latin America, and so forth.

CONTROLLED COMPOSITIONS

A key provision in any record agreement is known as a *controlled composition clause*. Such clauses are hard to avoid except by major recording artists. This clause is related to mechanical royalties. Many record labels insist that any song written by the producer and/or artist shall be a controlled composition. Labels prefer to put a cap (limit) on how much they have to pay to use a song, because unlike artist royalties, labels generally do not recoup advances, recording costs, and so on from mechanicals. Therefore, in the record contract, labels will only offer a producer and/or artist what is called a "rate" on controlled compositions. This contractual language usually specifies that the label won't pay more than seven and a half times the single-composition statutory rate for all cuts combined on the album *no matter how many are actually included*. Of course, this is done to protect the label's profit margin and overall investment in the recording. It can lead to dire consequences when the artist records both controlled and noncontrolled compositions. The publishers of the noncontrolled compositions (i.e., songs on the record which the artist and/or producer didn't write) are, of course, not required to abide by the 75 percent language and may demand the 100 percent statutory rate. Since there is a total-album maximum of 10 songs times 75 percent of the minimum statutory rate, the artist's own mechanical royalties could be reduced even below 75 percent in some cases if the label

68.2¢	Album-royalty maximum payable by record company
−18.2¢	Two outside songs at 9.1¢ each
50¢	
÷ 8	The number of artist-written songs
6.25¢	Per-song royalty to artist/writer and publisher

Source: Brabec and Brabec, "Controlled Composition Clauses."

must pay the full statutory rate for any noncontrolled songs. The statutory rate used in these types of calculations is the minimum rate in effect at the time the album was delivered to the record label.[7]

CHOOSING A PUBLISHER

One of the most important decisions a songwriter makes is with whom to place his or her songs. There is so much at stake, and songwriters often have a multitude of reasonable questions: Will my song be placed with an artist. . . let alone a great one? Will the publisher promote my music effectively? Will I receive an accurate and timely accounting of my royalties due?

The writer/publisher relationship is ultimately one of trust, and if you don't trust a publisher, you shouldn't place your song with that company. If you've never been published before (or published by a publisher who wants to publish your music), just do your homework. Go to the publisher's website to find out how long they've been in business, how they present themselves online (professionally? "mom and pop"?), who their writers are, whether they are publicly or privately held, how big they are . . . and so on. Find out who some of their current songwriters are and seek out a few of those writers to see if they're satisfied with the service they've received from that publisher. Some of these things won't be immediately apparent, but with some digging you can find out. Also, bigger doesn't necessarily mean better. Sometimes even with a large publisher's power and deep pockets, your song(s) get lost in the shuffle, with little or no promotion (or released late). Smaller "boutique" publishing houses are often more attentive (and selective) toward what and whom they publish. Yet smaller publishers sometimes have fewer resources to promote and administer your songs effectively. So these factors are often trade-offs. It depends on what you're looking for. Again, do your homework and that will go a long way in developing a mutually beneficial and satisfying publishing relationship. Publishers need writers and vice versa, and when the relationship works well, it's golden.

Under no circumstances should *you* ever pay to have your music published. Period. If someone approaches you and offers to publish your song for a price, that publisher isn't a legitimate publisher but merely a vanity house that wants to take your money. Sure, that publisher may provide an engraved copy of your music and put it up on a website or two (and possibly even make a demonstration recording of it), but it's doubtful they're going to vigorously promote it (if at all) since they haven't invested in the song themselves. To find lists of reputable music publishers and/or more information about music publishing, visit the websites for MPA (Music Publishers Association: www.mpa.org); NMPA (National Music Publishers Association: www.nmpa.org); and the Church Music Publishers Association (www.cmpamusic.org).

CODA

The business of music publishing is an exciting and fulfilling enterprise and, at its best, provides wonderful music for the world. Songwriters who connect with successful music publishers are paving the way to making their dreams come true.

In the Mix: Self-Publishing—To Do or Not to Do

A common question traditional music publishers sometimes hear from novice songwriters is, "Why should I assign the ownership of my song to a publisher? In today's Internet age, I can reach the world from my laptop." That's a fair question, and every music publisher worth his or her salt should have some great answers for that. So here are some key reasons a songwriter should place his or her song with a music publisher:

1. *Distribution.* Although today's composer can theoretically expose his or her song to "the world" through the Internet, as we all know, the information highway is unbelievably crowded and getting enough people to beat a path to your virtual door is complicated, difficult, and potentially costly (especially if you want to make a decent living at songwriting). Reputable, established music publishers have long-standing digital and physical distribution networks that are often decades old and can bring immediate results in selling your song and making you money for it.
2. *Focus.* Songwriting is a primarily creative, "right-brain" function, while publishing is primarily a "left-brain" business function (although there are many creative elements to it, of course, especially in selecting great songs and working with creative types). It's somewhat

rare to find a songwriter who is 100 percent interested and has the full capacity to handle all the business aspects of publishing in addition to the creative aspects of songwriting. But more than that, it's really a matter of time and focus. Publishing and songwriting are two separate and distinct disciplines that require a devotion of time and focus to succeed at a level where one can make a living.

3. *Energy.* When a writer is engaged in self-publishing, often his or her creative energy is sapped because the writer is answering the phone, creating contracts, and so on and generally being distracted and drained with the day-to-day demands of running a business. Inevitably, his or her songwriting suffers.

4. *Contacts.* Established publishers take the time and money to exhibit at trade shows, belong to various publishing organizations, dialogue with other publishers and make deals with them, have long-standing relationships with record labels and the multitude of other music users . . . all to the mutual benefit of writer and publisher.

5. *Knowledge.* The best publishers are always in touch with their various trade organizations and peers to learn more about and stay on top of the ever-changing publishing landscape in order to best serve their writers and exploit their songs most effectively.

6. *Infrastructure.* A successful music publisher has solid systems in place that serve their writers and customers to get the music out to as large an audience as possible. This includes accounting, licensing, an excellent website, marketing and promotional plans, and, most importantly, the ability to create excellent demos of their songs to showcase the songs in the best possible light for the most music users.

There are certainly times when self-publishing is in order, such as when a songwriter has achieved such success that they have earned the negotiating chip of keeping all or a portion of their publishing. But in those cases, most often the songwriter's portion is administered by a traditional publisher, since the songwriter is seldom interested in handling the back-office publishing functions. The songwriter is (logically) ultimately more interested in writing his or her next hit song.

Bottom line: Find a great publisher and get your music out there to make an impact on lives!

NOTES

1. "Tin Pan Alley," Wikipedia, https://en.wikipedia.org/wiki/Tin_Pan_Alley.

2. "Song Plugger," Wikipedia, https://en.wikipedia.org/wiki/Song_plugger.

3. Pam Phillips and Andrew Surmani, *Copyright Handbook for Music Educators and Directors: A Practical, Easy-to-Read Guide* (Van Nuys, CA: Alfred Music, 2017).

4. Harry Fox Agency (HFA), "What Does HFA Do?" HarryFox.com, https://www.harryfox.com/publishers/what_does_hfa_do.html.

5. "Synchronization Rights," Wikipedia, https://en.wikipedia.org/wiki/Synchronization_rights.

6. "Synchronization Rights."

7. Todd Brabec and Jeff Brabec, "Controlled Composition Clauses," ASCAP .com, 2007, https://www.ascap.com/help/music-business-101/controlled-composition-clauses.

7

DYNAMITE OR DINOSAUR

Record Labels

You're a local band until you get a record contract, then all of
a sudden Bruce Springsteen is your competition.

—Sam Llanas, singer/guitarist/songwriter

Record labels walk hand in hand with music publishing and performance rights organizations (PROs) as the largest generators of revenue in the music business. Recorded music has always dominated the business of music and does to this day, despite its tumultuous recent past. And although the fortunes of record labels have at times been in question, they have fought and managed to prevent their extinction in the digital age and remain the best path and central core of delivering music to the masses.

IN THE BEGINNING . . .

Through decades of the modern recording business, the method of music delivery has clearly changed and evolved: Beginning with lacquered 78 RPM (revolutions per minute) records and then 45 RPM singles (see figure 7.1) to vinyl LP ("long-play") records to eight-track cartridges, cassettes, laser discs, and then compact discs sold through retailers, the early days of the record business were indeed the "golden age" of the sale of records.

Record company executives often refer to the 1990s as "the good old days" of the recording industry. And for good reason. The industry was booming. According to CNN, total revenue for music sales and licensing peaked at $14.6 billion in 1999. However, by 2009, according to the Recording Industry Association of America (RIAA), revenues had plummeted

Fig 7.1.   Sample Vinyl Records

to $6.3 billion. And the culprit of the steep decline clearly began with peer-to-peer file sharing, such as the then newly birthed Napster service, a company that offered illegal sharing of electronic music files for free—known as stealing in the legitimate, legal music business.[1]

With the advent of the Internet and the emergence of Napster, the record business changed practically overnight as sales took a nosedive. Any business model is in the dumpster the minute someone can easily steal your products with a microscopic chance of ever being caught and held accountable. And illegal file sharing is precisely what doused record business revenues as the act of file sharing caught fire. Consequently, since everyone was doing it without penalty, a culture among (especially young) music users was fostered that promoted the belief that music should be free.

Technology kept moving ahead, and although iTunes—a legal Internet retail store for purchasing music—had come into existence by 2001, the recording industry was still feeling the shock waves of a new paradigm. Reeling from technology the industry hadn't been proactive enough to see coming, record labels shuttered right and left, especially the small, independent labels. And although the major bleeding has stopped, the industry still hasn't caught up to the sales figures it experienced in the "good old days."

All of the illegal downloading had a ripple effect in the music business. Other revenue streams suffered (such as publishing and print music) since far fewer royalties were paid for music use now that so much of it was now being obtained for free.

However, countless legal battles later, Napster now offers music legally for a subscription fee. Many other legal streaming music subscription services have come about such as Spotify and Rhapsody. And as iTunes grew and caught on with the rampant sales of iPhones (and the music business picked itself up off the floor and got better at enforcing the copyright law against companies facilitating illegal downloading), the idea of "convergence" and "bundling" grew (i.e., the converging or bundling of two technologies with each other: phone and music, for example). The new, convenient (and legal) way of accessing music through phone apps caused the growth of legal downloads to flourish.

But legal downloads unfortunately didn't replace the lost revenues from the downward spiral of physical CD sales, leading to further (and often massive) cutbacks in record label staffs and budgets. Still, as stated earlier, record labels have continued to claw their way into continued relevance and existence by staying on top of the digital age (or more accurately, playing catch-up), along with expanding their reach into an artist's revenue streams by doing "360 deals" (more on those later).

Those streaming services such as the aforementioned Spotify, plus Amazon, SoundCloud, Apple Music, and others, have made music an even more perishable commodity by putting it totally in "the cloud" and not residing even as downloaded MP3 files on one's computer or phone. However, the ubiquity of these and other streaming services has had a distinct upside for recorded music by making it all the more available to almost everyone. For example, in 2016, according to the RIAA, streams of songs made up a whopping 51 percent of all U.S. music revenues (with a staggering 432 *billion* songs streamed on demand in 2016).[2] And record labels were at the center of all the fun and excitement. (Though the complaint from record companies, artists, and music publishers alike to this bumper crop of billions of streams is that the revenues generated from them fall painfully short of what they once made on physical CD or album sales . . . or even downloads, making the challenge of monetizing music consumption still harder than ever.)

We can add another little wild card into the mix: the return of physical vinyl LPs as a viable, desirable revenue stream for the record industry. Those sales hit a twenty-eight-year high in 2016, with young listeners and millennials, who will theoretically continue to be music buyers their entire lives, embracing the format.[3] Will many of them want to buy vinyl records in the future as well? Such buying habits only increase the challenge and futility of foretelling the ultimate future of the record business.

TODAY'S MODERN RECORD LABELS

As it has been in the past, a record label's job is to exploit their record-ings, regardless of the format. It doesn't matter if the master sound re-cordings are offered in a digital, streaming, or physical format. Remem-ber, master recordings are copyrighted separately from songs, as discussed in chapter 6. The circled *C* (©) standing for *copyright* is different from the circled *P* (℗), which stands for *phonorecord*, as noted earlier. So a record company copyrights the master recording. No one can use that master without permission from the owner of the master (most often the record company). Some artists may own their masters, if they can afford it and so desire.

In the early days of the record business, artists or songwriters rarely, if ever, owned their master recordings or even recorded their own songs. (Then along came the Beatles, who also wrote many of their songs and, thanks to their enormous popularity as artists, they didn't need a publisher per se to exploit and pitch their songs to other artists in order to generate revenue from them. The Beatles changed a lot of things about the music business, and this was one of the most significant changes.) Prior to the ar-rival of that boy band from across the pond, record labels would pay large sums of money to finance and own the master recordings, in addition to the extravagant cost of pressing and shipping potentially millions of LPs. These labels often were the record distributors as well, thus controlling the destiny of the artist completely.

But in today's record business, with the digital realm ruling, the tra-ditional record business model has been upended. Artists can compose and record a song on a digital audio workstation (DAW), such as FL Studio or Ableton. They can then mix it themselves and do all this relatively inex-pensively in a home studio. Labels still have to find talent and help launch or maintain careers, but their focus and power nowadays is more on the marketing and promotional side of the recording. And most labels have the money to make this happen, securing feature placements on iTunes and Beatport, inclusion in Spotify playlists, press coverage on blogs and magazines, and plugging recordings to radio. That's where the proverbial "rubber meets the road."

Record labels today are busier than ever exploiting their masters in all formats available, including physical formats, until the foreseeable future when that format completely disappears. The death of the physical format has been predicted for years, and most see it as inevitable, but on the other hand, who could have foreseen the resurgence of vinyl records?

In an effort to make ends meet with the decline of physical record sales, many record labels have engaged for several years in the now-popular "360 deal." Such a deal is a contract between artist and label wherein the label is responsible for handling all (or most) aspects of the artist's career (i.e., 360 degrees) of that career. Not only does the label provide recording support and financing, but it also provides tour, merchandise, and other promotional support. In addition, if the record label has a music publisher contained under its roof (and most labels do), the label will procure a deal with the artist who is also a songwriter (as most are these days) to control all (or at least a portion) of that artist's publishing revenues and administration.

RECORD COMPANY STRUCTURE

Record companies come in all shapes and sizes . . . from one-person operations with part-time employees (distributed by a larger company) to "the Big Three":

- Sony BMG
- Universal Music Group
- Warner Music Group

There used to be four major labels—EMI was once one of them—but Universal Music purchased EMI in 2012. So where once there were the Big Four, now there's just the Big Three. These companies make up almost 80 percent of the music market or even more depending on the year, although it was estimated to be about two-thirds in 2016 (according to Nielsen SoundScan figures).[4] The rest of the market is composed of independent labels.

Within a major or medium-sized record label, you will find the following positions:

1. Upper Management (CEO, COO, CFO, President, etc.)

The "executive suite" in medium and larger labels contains all, some, or more of these roles: CEO (chief executive officer)/president, COO (chief operating officer), and CFO (chief financial officer). Larger labels often have a CMO (chief marketing officer) and CCO (chief creative officer). These are the ultimate leaders of the company, providing vision and creative/management direction for the label.

2. A&R—Artists and Repertoire

An individual who serves as A&R has the role of finding and nurturing talent. Then, once that talent is found and signed to the label, the A&R person has to match the right songs to that performer. In that respect, the A&R person's role is akin to a casting agent for a movie. The person who is in A&R for a label must be keenly aware of music trends, what's charting on the music charts, and be "ahead of the curve" for what is commercially viable and what is not. At the same time, A&R people need to have excellent people skills and be able to work closely with artists whose career they have as their main priority. Sometimes, they may need to coax and convince an artist to move in a direction that is in the best interest of the artist based on current commercial trends, yet never push the artist to a place that can't be an ultimate fit with who that artist is. Music business history is replete with examples of artists and labels who parted ways because they could no longer find common ground as music trends changed and the artist wasn't interested in or capable of changing with the times. Therefore, being a "market researcher" and in tune with where the label's chosen market lies is an important part of this role.

3. Distribution

The function of music distribution has changed a great deal with the advent of digital distribution. Accordingly, physical distribution of records has diminished greatly as digital downloads and streaming are the main choice for today's music consumer. The Big Three record labels have their own distribution systems and also distribute recordings for numerous owned and independent labels, but even they have seen a tremendous reduction in the amount of physical products that are being sold these days.

That said, physical distribution of CDs and vinyl records is not completely extinct . . . yet. But most of the music business intelligentsia agree and predict that there will be some sort of physical product available in the foreseeable future, however how large that market will be is unclear.

The (what now seems old-fashioned) manner of manufacturing CDs involves sending the master recording to a CD duplicator along with artwork for the container. CD manufacturers still offer a variety of packaging types: jewel case (the most typical type of packaging), slim line (not as thick as a jewel case), cardboard sleeve with or without a flap, paper sleeves with a window (to see the "raw" CD imprint), and plastic clamshell (with a number of multiple disc configurations). If there is separate printed material that is inserted into a jewel case, the labels send the press-ready artwork to the CD manufacturer for printing. This includes a CD booklet or one- to two-page insert plus a tray card (the part that is placed beneath the plastic CD holder, which is tightly snapped into place in the jewel case). Vinyl records have their own process, which varies greatly from CD manufacturing, but the principles of manufacturing a disc and placing it in a printed holder are the same as with a CD.

After the CD or vinyl record is manufactured, it is shipped to the label's warehouse (or the label's distributor) for distribution coast to coast and around the world.

Digital distribution is traditionally handled by the same entity that distributes that physical products. All major labels have direct agreements with the largest digital service providers (DSPs) such as iTunes, Spotify, and Beatport. There are some companies that offer automated digital distribution, such as TuneCore, DistroKid, or CD Baby (although CD Baby offers a mix of digital and physical products if desired by the record label). Most small independent labels nowadays offer digital distribution only; no physical products. Not having physical products certainly reduces the liability of having money tied up in inventory on warehouse shelves. This also reduces returns. Returns occur when physical merchandise doesn't "sell through" at the retail store level . . . meaning that for whatever reason(s), the customers just didn't purchase it. And labels traditionally offer retailers the option to return the unsold merchandise for full credit. Sometimes record labels will require sales of their products to be "one-way sales" (meaning no returns allowed), but those types of sales usually only happen on heavily discounted or closeout, liquidation titles.

For their services, physical distributors of products generally take anywhere from 15 percent (very low side) to 30 percent (high side) of net sales in exchange for distributing and promoting products and depending on the extent of the services they offer. For example, *fulfillment* is a component of distribution, but product fulfillment and *distribution* are not the same. Fulfillment involves retrieving (by a person from the warehouse shelf when an order is placed), packing, and shipping the products. Distribution includes the fulfillment element but adds sales and marketing. When physical record sales were booming, the major record labels (and even major independent labels) had large sales teams . . . in-house on the phone (receiving inbound and making outbound calls), as well as road representatives ("road reps") who visited retail stores in person. The days of road reps are mostly over, with only a handful of phone reps left to service retail accounts.

Digital distributors generally receive between 10 percent to 15 percent of net sales. Their percentage is lower since they don't have the expense of a physical warehouse.

How a label is distributed and its reach and sales performance in the marketplace is certainly often a deciding factor on whether or not a particular artist signs with that label.

4. Music Promotion

After creating outstanding products, the promotion of recordings in a record label's catalog is arguably the most important activity the label carries out. Clearly, marketing drives sales. Without aggressive marketing, especially in today's overcrowded marketplace, a new recording is most likely doomed to failure.

The most common way to promote new albums these days remains radio. But that medium has seen a big transformation as well in the previous decades. However, radio is still a powerful tool in reaching people. Terrestrial (AM and FM) radio still plays a significant role on the media landscape today. According to a recent report by the Nielsen Company,

> radio leads all other platforms when it comes to weekly reach (93%) among adult consumers—and with new insights available to compare radio to other platforms on a regular basis, it's clear that radio is an integral part of media consumption for millions of Americans.
>
> Today the words "radio" and "audio" mean many different things to many different people: music, commentary, podcasting, digital listening, in-car entertainment and on and on. What's certain is that the radio consumer is a highly qualified audience, delivered in real-time across hundreds of markets every single day. Most radio listeners are in the workforce and are reached when they're away from home and ready to buy.
>
> In a time of intense competition for audience attention, radio reaches more Americans each week than any other platform. Ninety-three percent of adult consumers (18+) use radio on a weekly basis, more than TV or smartphones.[5]

The goal for all record labels is that record stations will put their record (or more likely, single song from that record) into constant or "heavy" rotation, meaning it's played regularly and frequently. This leads to chart action and sales online and at the retail level. Promotional departments or persons at labels seek to get exposure to their artists and songs on music blogs, magazines, feature placements on iTunes and Spotify, interviews on television and radio shows, let alone the artist's touring that comes with a new record. Social media also plays a major role these days, now more than ever, in the successful promotion of music. YouTube is also a major way to get exposure for the artist and his or her music.

There are third-party agencies that do nothing but specialize in the promotion of music on behalf of record labels. Small, independent labels rely on such agencies since they seldom have the staffing available or an in-house promotional department, as with major record labels.[6]

5. Publicists and PR Agencies

In addition to promotional departments and/or agencies, a key element of music promotion includes *publicists* and *PR* (public relations) specialists. These people are responsible for garnering positive press attention, both online and offline (print, broadcast). Their job is to get as much "buzz" generated about a new release and its artist(s) as possible. They can be engaged not only by record labels but also by artists themselves, event promoters, and venue owners. The best publicists write and distribute "clean" (mistake-free) press releases on time and well in advance of an album release. They are detail oriented and help generate exclusive and first-rate opportunities for the artist and label. This is all done for an agreed-upon advance fee or on a per-project basis.[7]

6. Radio Pluggers

Radio pluggers are also referred to as *radio promoters* or *song pluggers*. These are the people who must decide which stations to approach whose music format is the most appropriate in promoting their label's recording. They build relationships with as many stations as possible but particularly with *reporting stations*. These are the stations that the trade papers, song-tracking services, and other measurement methods look to learn which songs are being programmed on a weekly, monthly, and yearly basis. The plugger's goal is to get songs they're plugging placed into rotation. Pluggers are either independent or employees of record labels (in the radio department) or PR agencies. Major labels generally have multiple pluggers focus on respective territories throughout the United States and Canada and even international territories.[8]

If you are a budding artist, finding out all you can about a potential label's radio promotion department is a good move: Do they have an in-house promotional department or do they use an outside agency? What sort of budget would they be able to devote to promoting your record?

Again, it's all about relationships. In the case of Internet and satellite radio, radio/song plugging is done very similarly as with terrestrial radio, and that's through relationships developed . . . independently or as an employee of a record label.

7. Business and Legal Affairs

This department of a typical record label handles all the contracts (incoming and outgoing) for the label. These include artist agreements, licensing use of their masters, procuring mechanical licenses, and so forth. Accounting and other financial functions for the company (cash flow statements and projections, etc.) also flow through this area. (Larger labels often have a separate accounting department.)

8. Special Products

Larger record labels often include this division, which focuses on the catalog of the company. In publishing, a catalog is the body of copyrights contained in the publisher. In the record business, the catalog is the vault of masters contained in the company. This vault is a record company's lifeblood, and it behooves the company to exploit those masters on a continual basis in every way possible: repackaging them in "best of" compilations, budget and "mid-price" or "midline" repackaging, television and movie placement, and so forth.

9. Merchandise

With the advent of 360 deals, labels have a direct stake in artist merchandise revenues. Artist merchandise (or "merch") has become a significant generator of revenues for labels, and there are countless creative ways to generate money (while expanding an artist's branding). Apparel and posters are the natural pieces of merch, but key chains, insulated drinking cups, or jewelry are other examples of additional merch items. Sometimes the purchase of physical merch brings with it additional digital "goodies" (such as an MP3 file of a single song) or vice versa (such as a T-shirt with the purchase of a digital album).

10. International

Foreign selling for record labels has always been a major source of revenues for record labels. These departments make sure the sales channels between the U.S. headquarters and any international affiliates are open and communicating effectively. Different time zones and distance offer their own challenges, but those are easily handled when one or more people within the label focus on international sales. Major labels can glean up to 50 percent of their total revenue from international territories when they are serviced correctly.

11. Publishing

Most record labels have in-house publishing departments (again, especially with the rise of the 360 deal). As noted in chapter 6, music publishing can be very lucrative, and record labels are eager to leverage every aspect of their artists' talents. With so many artists also acting as songwriters these days, it makes sense for a record label to also have an in-house publishing division. The label sets up two or three publishing companies (for their ASCAP, BMI, and SESAC writers, respectively) and accounts for the revenue generated by these publishers are kept separate from their record business. However, since the publishers are ultimately still a part of the overall company's revenues, there can be a possibility for the record division to make "sweetheart" deals with the publishing company (e.g., the publishing division offering the record division a reduced mechanical rate on songs for no good reason other than to fatten up the company's bottom line). In such a case as this, the songwriter is the one who loses out on his or her writer's share of the mechanical royalty, so it's important for writers to pay attention to their royalty statements and make sure they're not getting the short end of the stick. Reputable music publishers never do such sweetheart deals at the expense of their writers.

THE RECORDING ACADEMY

The Recording Academy (formerly named the National Academy of Recording Arts and Sciences or NARAS) is a U.S. organization of musicians, producers, recording engineers, and other recording professionals. Headquartered in Santa Monica, California, it's best known as the presenter/owner of the annual Grammy Awards.[9] Members of the Recording Academy select the Grammy winners each year. The Grammys are the only peer-presented award to honor artistic achievement, technical proficiency, and overall excellence in the recording industry"[10]

The Recording Academy's 12 regional chapters represent music markets coast to coast. The chapters work all year long to build community through professional development programming, panel discussions, informative email blasts, helpful website content, networking, advocacy, and philanthropy. The chapters are located in Atlanta, Chicago, Miami (Florida), Los Angeles, Memphis, Nashville, New York, Portland (Pacific Northwest), Philadelphia, San Francisco, Austin (Texas), and Washington, DC. [11]

THE FUTURE

The modern recording business is alive (and yes, well) and relevant today as it continues to provide today's artists with a variety of means by which to share their talents with as broad a market as possible. It's doubtful that some form of record labels—be it major, indie, digital only or whatever future form of delivery may be conceived—won't exist in the future, and the record labels of tomorrow will continue to defy extinction.

For the would-be future record-label employee, the outlook for labels is positive overall based on the fact that many labels—major or independent—are still surviving and, in many cases, thriving. Whether you choose to seek employment at a major or independent label depends largely on what position(s) might be available when you go looking for a job. But generally, the best opportunities are at smaller, growing independent labels that offer experience in a wide number of areas (since smaller shops have fewer people doing more things).

Internships are the best entrance into a label, since interns—after proving themselves—are often the first considered for entry-level paying positions. However, it's best not to try to gain an internship unless you're enrolled in a college or university since companies are often reluctant to bring someone in who isn't under the auspices of such an institution (and therefore held accountable for showing up on time, doing a good job, etc., since the intern will receive a review and grade). Paid internships aren't unheard of but are very rare.

If you aren't in a position to do an internship, then landing a job at a record label without prior experience can be difficult (though certainly not impossible!). Three words will help you do so: network, network, network. And if you have a solid track record with a previous employer along with great recommendations (regardless of what industry it is in), you may have a chance at landing an entry- or mid-level position at a record label. You can position yourself as a "blank slate," ready and willing to learn the business the record label's way, without any baggage of "we did it another way" at another label.

NOTES

1. David Goldman, "Music's Lost Decade: Sales Cut in Half," CNNMoney .com, http://money.cnn.com/2010/02/02/news/companies/napster_music_in dustry/.

2. Joshua P. Friedlander, *News and Notes on 2017 RIAA Revenue Statistics* (Washington, DC: Recording Industry Association of America, 2018), http:// www.riaa.com/wp-content/uploads/2018/03/RIAA-Year-End-2017-News-and -Notes.pdf.

3. Cary Sherman, "RIAA Presidential Report" (presented at the 2018 Church Music Publishers Association Convention, Fort Lauderdale, FL, April 10–13, 2018).

4. Nielsen, *2016 U.S. Music Year-End Report*, Nielsen.com, January 9, 2017, http://www.nielsen.com/us/en/insights/reports/2017/2016-music-us-year-end -report.html.

5. Nielsen, "Audio Today: Radio 2016—Appealing Far and Wide," Nielsen .com, February 25, 2016, http://www.nielsen.com/us/en/insights/reports/2016/ audio-today-radio-2016-appealing-far-and-wide.html.

6. Budi Voogt, "Understanding the Music Industry: Records Labels, A&Rs, Distribution, Pluggers and PR," Heroic Academy, February 27, 2017, https://heroic.aca demy/understanding-music-industry-record-labels-ars-distribution-pluggers-pr/.

7. Voogt, "Understanding the Music Industry."

8. Voogt, "Understanding the Music Industry."

9. "The Recording Academy," Wikipedia, https://en.wikipedia.org/wiki/ The_Recording_Academy.

10. Recording Academy, "About the Recording Academy," Grammy.com, https://www.grammy.com/recording-academy/about.

11. Recording Academy, "Chapters," Grammy.com, https://www.grammy .com/recording-academy/chapters.

8

MAKING IT RAIN

Revenue Streams

If we do our job . . . music's not black or white, it's green.

—Jim Caparro

If you love to make music . . . or simply love music and want to be associated with it one way or another every day and garner your livelihood
from it . . . there's nothing better than getting up every day to *make a living
making music!* The best jobs are the ones where you think you're not "going to work" but merely doing what you do each day as an extension of
who you are deep inside yourself. But finding a way to make a full-time
living in the music business can be difficult (especially nowadays; see figure
8.1). Through the years, many people who want to make money making
music do it by cobbling together a number of smaller music jobs (gigging
musician; teaching; songwriting; playing at churches, weddings, nightclubs,
drama productions, etc.), and that's certainly a viable approach. Others seek
full-time employment at a music publisher, record label, performance rights
organization (PRO), and so forth (and if they're also practicing musicians,
they find the time and energy to play gigs after hours in their spare time).
Of course, that's also a very desirable and fulfilling path. The bottom line
is that although it can be tough to make a living making music, the good
news is that in some ways, there have never been more ways to do it. For
the resourceful person who is energetic and filled with "hustle," one can
fulfill one's music dream and turn it into green.

So where does all the money *really* come from? How can one make
money change hands in exchange for using one's musical and/or administ-
trative and business talents? Beginners in the music business are sometimes
confused about from which source(s) money flows for the music business

Fig 8.1.   The State of the Music Business. *Illustration by Richard Duszczak*

and how that flow actually works. Novice artists and songwriters, for example, sometimes think that merely by practicing their craft, someone somewhere (usually a large record or publishing company) will show up magically and start paying them to make music simply because they're good at it. But the truth is that there are countless people in the world who are good (and great) at making music and never make a dime from it—either by choice (e.g., they want music to be a hobby) or because they don't quite know how the "dots" are connected to make money making music.

In its most basic form, the music business revenue stream involves getting songs to consumers. Period. Creative people create (write songs, sing, and/or play) and the "music business machine" gets those songs to the world of consumers (see figure 8.2).

When we unpack the "cogs and wheels" of the music business machine, we see it takes an army of people, companies, and processes to get music to the public:

- Songwriters (plus arrangers and orchestrators)
- Music publishers
- Record labels
- Performing rights organizations
- Producers
- Personal managers
- Business managers
- Agents
- Attorneys
- Recording engineers
- Performers and recording artists/recording session (studio) musicians
- Touring musicians
- Brand-related merchandise
- Crowd/fan/corporate funding
- Music retailers
- Music teachers
- Religious services
- Arts administrators

Fig 8.2. The Music Business Machine

Money is the "grease" that keeps the wheels turning in the music business. And as with any big machine, the wheels are most often interlocked and depend on each other to move and make things happen.

Where might you fit into the machine? How can you use your best and most enjoyed skills to make a living in the music industry? If you're already a part of the music business machine, how might you make a change and/or broaden your scope of influence and revenue if so desired? You needn't move to one of the major music centers in the United States (New York, Los Angeles, or Nashville) . . . although that certainly doesn't hurt. You can do it right where you are. So let's further unpack the elements of the music business machine to investigate the available opportunities and what is involved with each.

Songwriters (plus arranging and orchestrating). As stated previously in this book, "It all begins with a song." The art and craft of songwriting has already been discussed in chapter 2 but not the process/role of an arranger/orchestrator.

As an *arranger*, the primary role is to artfully arrange or organize the melodies and harmonies provided by the composer into a solidly realized piece of music. Some composers come to the table with arranging ideas in mind; others only show up with a lead sheet that has verse/chorus/verse/chorus on it. The arranger's job is to bring that song to life. The arranger will write an introduction and perhaps some interludes between verses. The arranger may slightly tweak some of the composer's original harmonies (with the permission of the composer, of course) to enrich them all the more. The arranger may even slightly alter the melody if any altered harmonies are suggested (but again, *only* with the composer's permission prior to arranging the piece). The arranger may sometimes even change the structure of the piece. The arranger should always honor and respect the composer's original intent for the piece, and only act as a "creative facilitator" to enrich the composer's original melody and harmonies through the arranger's own creative efforts. It can be a bit of a dance, if you will, between composer and arranger, but a careful and collaborative dance that is borne out of respect and musicianship.[1]

An *orchestrator* is a trained musician who assigns which instrument plays which notes in the song or work. For example, the orchestrator of a Broadway musical plays an integral part in a show's sound (read more about writing for the theatre in chapter 10). The composer(s) writes the score, then the orchestrator comes along and decides which instrument will play which part of the melody and other parts of the chords in the overall harmonic structure. But the art of orchestration goes much further than that. The orchestrator also often adds various new background and "filler" melodic embellishments and countermelodies to complement, enrich, and enhance the overall effect of the music (while never crowding or changing the composer's original music and intent). Great orchestrations are like herbs and spices that bring out the best in food. Top orchestrators also understand the nuances and capabilities of each orchestral instrument and how to blend those instruments seamlessly while making them sound their best. Orchestrating is not arranging in the sense where an arranger can change the structure of a piece. The orchestrator's job is never to make those types of changes but to enrich what is already there.

The structure and functions of *music publishers*, *record companies*, and *performing rights organizations* have been discussed elsewhere in this book. For the purposes of this chapter, we'll consider the environments of each and how that may or may not make them attractive as a place to pursue your dreams.

Surprisingly enough, *music publishing* offices are not always alive with the sound of music. They are more likely to be humming with computer sounds and people clicking away on keyboards as they create contracts or calculate royalties. Add to that one or more employees who either speak on the phone with or email songwriters who have solicited songs to be published. Those employees give the songwriters valuable feedback on their submissions. Most importantly, certain employees are also always involved in pitching songs to users of music (film, television, print, etc.). Actual music making does come in the form of making demos of the songs a publisher has signed. That's done in a small, in-house studio or an inexpensive one nearby. Or perhaps a songwriter plays a "scratch vocal" demo made in a bedroom studio for the publisher, hoping said publisher will sign it.

On the other hand, *record labels* are often teeming with music sounds emitting from their offices throughout the day, since A&R (artists and repertoire) people and executives are listening to those demos created by music publishers to determine if they would like to have one of their artists record the song. They're also listening to rough or final mixes of their artists' latest recording to approve what an in-house or freelance producer has created for them. Or perhaps they are listening to a competitor's top-selling song to try and decipher the "secret sauce" that made that particular tune the latest hit. There are a lot of computers humming and clicking here too.

Performing rights organizations (PROs) offer relatively limited opportunities for employment in the grand scheme of things since there are only three major ones in the United States (see figure 8.3). That said, however, each of them employs a large number of people in multiple offices, so if you're interested in this substantial branch or "cog" of the music business, PROs offer a variety of opportunities. From meeting with songwriters to crunching numbers on computers to licensing new businesses to be legal users of music from the PRO's respective repertoires, PROs help keep the music alive.

Aside from composers and arrangers, *producers* can also have a major impact on the final product. Producers use their extensive musical abilities and studio experience to help shape the overall sound of the recording. From the original recording session to mixing, mastering, and editing, producers oversee the entire process, including budgeting. And although not all producers have degrees in music, it's useful to have one (or at least be able to read music) since a producer needs always to know the score (literally).

Producing is an art. Whether producing a solo artist, four-member band, children's ensemble, or full orchestra, producers need to know

Fig 8.3. PRO Logos

how to motivate and coax the very best performance out of their talent. Sometimes that means being part psychologist to "read" the talent's mood and energy level. Other times it means being a creative type in order to come up with an alternate ending on the spot since the one that is written down isn't working. The producer needs to balance all of those things while keeping an eye on the clock, because as the old saying goes, "time is money!" Indeed, this is true in the studio, since you're probably paying for studio time (and not using your cousin's home studio for free), the talent, the engineer, and recording materials. Those costs add up fast (especially if you have a full orchestra sitting on the floor). On top of all of that, a producer is most concerned with what ultimately ends up on the recording and that it's right . . . technically, sonically, and musically. Finally, a producer must juggle all these balls and hopefully keep a cheerful and professional attitude, even in the face of the occasional technical glitch, which inevitably happens. The producer must keep his or her cool even if time starts to get tight and it looks as though the session might not finish on time. If the producer is nervous or "short" with his or her talent and/or engineer, it can put a cloud of tension over the session, which makes it harder to feel free to make great music. Although that all sounds like a tall order, producing can be one of the most satisfying, invigorating, and thrilling parts of the music business.

Personal managers are often the most important member of the artist's team. Personal managers advise and guide their clients' professional choices. For example, when faced with multiple offers for competing projects, the personal manager helps the client decide which is potentially the best choice. Personal managers often serve as a bridge between a record label's A&R manager and the artist. For example, if an artist is interested in working with a particular producer, the personal manager might approach the recording label's A&R head to move such a deal forward. There are countless other choices an artist makes in his or her career (tour decisions, business investment decisions, etc.). The personal manager stands ready to help guide the artist's decisions.[2]

Business managers represent artists, musicians, and writers in business matters that relate to their career. That includes financial calculations as well, such as tax returns, royalty statements/payment accuracy, investments, accounting, and negotiating. The business manager is arguably the most important person on an artist's team or career. Depending on the scope of the artist's career, a business manager may represent multiple clients. Music business superstars are artists who not only need but can afford a business manager all to themselves. Business managers obviously need a solid background in business (and accounting as well), preferably with a degree in business administration. The best business managers help chart a path of financial success for their clients . . . both short term and long term.[3]

Attorneys draft contracts and help their clients understand incoming and outgoing contracts, ensuring that the terms are in their clients' best interests. They work with artists, bands, producers, songwriters, music publishers, record label executives . . . basically everyone and anyone in the music business. When serving artists, songwriters, and/or producers, attorneys do everything from negotiating contracts (recording, merchandising, touring, and publishing) to constructing contracts from scratch when a client needs to have a contract created. When serving a record label or publisher, they fill the crucial role of helping set up a new business, act as an advisor to purchase another company, or help in arbitrating a dispute.[4]

Recording engineers are much more than just "knob jockeys"(!). They are the producer's best friend in any recording session. The producer depends on the engineer first and foremost to make sure that what is going onto the recording is sonically and technically accurate and correct; that all that is being recorded is recorded in the best, most economical way. The engineer chooses the microphones, sets recording levels, and makes many subtle sound manipulation decisions (often unbeknownst to the producer, since the really deep technical things are often beyond a producer's purview, knowledge, or interest). The best engineers are often also musicians and always have a great set of ears to "hear the grass grow" as some say. But having a natural interest, ability, and training for the technical and computer aspects of the recording process is also a must.[5]

Knowing when to speak up to a producer when he or she perceives something as wrong (or not speak up) is a skill as well, since no producer wants to feel as if his or her judgement is being usurped in the recording process. However, most producers will welcome strategic comments from the engineer if he or she is hearing a problem in the recording process that the producer happens to miss in the heat of the moment during a busy, sometimes pressure-packed session.

The actual music making on a recording naturally falls on the shoulders of *performers* and *recording artists*. Band and solo artist performing careers are covered elsewhere in this book, so we'll specifically consider *studio musicians* in this context. These often-unsung heroes of the music business are the background singers and instrumentalists who come into a session and often sight-read the music (or "chart") and then are recorded. If you're a singer or player with enormous "chops" (a superior ability to accurately sight-read music and perform for recording), then the life of a studio musician could be for you. These musicians often belong to the AFM (American Federation of Musicians) so not only do they receive fair compensation for their time and talents, they also receive additional perks (such as retirement benefits).

Professional music performers also come in the shape of symphony orchestra performers. These players often belong to the AFM, and although symphony positions can be very hard to come by, once a job is landed, it can be a wonderful means of making a living. According to the League of American Orchestras, there are 1,200 symphony orchestras in the United States.[6] The larger the city in which the orchestra is based, the more difficult to get a permanent position with one. For example, it's harder to land a position with the Chicago Symphony Orchestra or the New York Philharmonic (since the gig pays much more and the competition is fiercer) than a symphony based in a city of 50,000 people or less. But no permanent symphony gig is an easy one to procure. As the old joke goes, when a stranger asks directions of another stranger on the streets of New York City: "How do I get to Carnegie Hall?," the other replies, "Practice, man, practice!"

Performers and recording artists often *tour*, and touring not only affords its own lifestyle but has always been an important revenue stream in the music business. With the decline of physical record sales, now more than ever touring is a vital piece of revenue. It's impossible to illegally download the actual experience of a live concert event. Sure, fans can illegally record a concert on their phone and then share it online, but for the viewer of such a video, it's still not the same as being there.

Artists and record labels get a percentage of the "gate" (box office revenues) on a tour. Tour support money paid out by the record label is usually recouped (at least 50 percent) before the artist sees any money from the box office receipts, however.

With any performing group, the experience of living as a touring musician will vary greatly from city to city and tour to tour. Artists or groups travel by bus, RV, plane, or even train. Touring is obviously a great way to see new places. Larger tours with headline artists or groups allow many other people/nonmusicians to meet and interact. During the travel time between cities, if it's going to take several days to get to the next location, some artists use that time to visit home or take a minivacation.

The flip side of being able to take a minivacation is when there are so many shows and the commute to the venue can be so long that there's literally no time for anything but eating, sleeping, and performing. Since you're always on the road when touring, equipment breakdowns sometimes happen. That can mean no water or electricity or sitting still for hours on the road. Internet and phone service can sometimes disappear for weeks at a time. Unless you're a major band or solo artist, living space can be tiny, and if you haven't brought enough to entertain yourself, you might get a touch of cabin fever. Worst of all, sometimes beginning artists go through a lot of trouble and expend a lot of energy to put on a two-hour show, only to have the audience barely applaud or acknowledge their efforts. But of course, as the appreciation and popularity of an artist grows, the applause and attendance can be staggering and intoxicating.

Most touring musicians do what they do because they love it, while for major artists it's expected and a must to get their music out there. This often requires the sacrifice of family time, vacations, and personal comfort to pursue that passion. Being on tour can be difficult, but it also can be really fun and a once-in-a-lifetime experience.

On any tour, there's always *brand-related merchandise* on sale somewhere at the venue. This "merch"—as it's called—can be a lucrative part of the revenue stream for any artist—and record label, since these days with 360 deals, labels often have a hand in that pocket. Usually, merch manufacture and sales are hired out to a *merchandiser*. That company manufactures the goods, such as apparel (T-shirts, hoodies, scarves, etc.), souvenirs (posters, coffee mugs, artist programs and/or pictures, keychains, etc.), or other creative products, which most often reflect the uniqueness of the artist. These items are for sale on a table or booth at the concert, usually with a substantial markup. Of course, physical CDs (or even vinyl albums) from the artist are always one of the biggest sellers at the merch table. The merchandiser accounts to the artist or record company for all sales and pays a royalty for those sales. There's *a name/image/likeness (NIL) royalty* attached to each product that is sold (generally 5 percent of the retail price). This NIL royalty is also paid on print music folios where the artist's name, image, and likeness are used.

Most, if not all, of these merch items are available for sale at a physical retail location or online (especially on the artist's and/or label's website), but when the fan is at the concert and gets swept up in the live performance element, that fuels merch to sell much better at the live event versus retail, which is obviously removed from the live experience.

Crowd/fan/corporate funding is yet another revenue stream that keeps the music business machine oiled and running. Crowd funding involves the person(s) who desires funding using a web-based platform such as Kickstarter. For example, a band may need money to fund their first (or latest) recording. Through direct-to-fan marketing (social media, email, direct contact at concerts, etc.), the artist or band makes a pitch to their fans to contribute to their recording. In exchange (based on the level of contribution), the fans receive premiums (a free download and/or physical copy of the recording for a $50 donation; a free download and/or physical copy of the recording plus a T-shirt for a $75 donation, etc.). In addition to Kickstarter, some of the current crowd-funding platforms are ArtistShare, Indiegogo, PledgeMusic, and RocketHub.

Since the advent of the Internet, *music retailers* have been challenged in a way never seen before. It started with the likes of Amazon and iTunes replacing many of the brick-and-mortar retailers of the world and was followed by the usurping of magazines by music blogs and social media. In addition, music retail has witnessed the incursion of online subscription services like Spotify and Deezer that further displace the need for downloadable content, let alone physical products purchased from retailers.

Retail disruption was lifted to higher levels with social media being used as a direct-to-fan marketing tool that puts the artist in direct contact with their global fan base. It means a touring band or artist can outsell traditional outlets, all with a tweet and an email and at a marketing cost that is minimal.

So have music retailers folded their tents? Not yet! And most likely, never. In the next chapter, music retailing (physical and digital) is examined more closely, as it remains a very important piece of the puzzle in getting music out to the world. For the purposes of this chapter, however, and what it's like to work for a music retailer, it's certainly still a very viable career choice, provided you carefully select the music retailer, of course. Make sure you align with a retailer that has a solid track record of reasonable success and stability. This can be determined by talking to customers and considering your own experience as a customer with that retailer. When you visit the store, what is the overall "vibe"? Is it organized or in disarray? Is there a lot of store traffic, or is it more like a ghost town? Do they have an up-to-date, modern, and user-friendly website? Finally, are the management and sales clerks friendly, approachable, knowledgeable, and seemingly happy to be there? The list could go on, but you get the idea. With some careful research and homework, the truth is usually hiding in plain sight. As with most retail environments, you'll probably be asked to work extended hours or weekends occasionally. But helping a customer find the perfect product to make great music is worth it!

Being a *music teacher* is a career choice that isn't for everyone. But if sharing your passion and joy for music with those who want to learn from you also gives you joy, then being a music teacher can be a rewarding,

Fig 8.4. Music Education Grading. *Illustration by Richard Duszczak*

stable, and steady career path. Discovering if you are cut out to become a teacher sometimes happens early in life by realizing you like working with children and/or finding you enjoy sharing knowledge with someone who is learning it for the first time. You might even realize you enjoy grading exams! Teaching is the ultimate way to give oneself and one's art away to benefit others, while possibly leaving a legacy for generations to come through passing on one's musical knowledge and life experiences.

However, securing a music teaching job has never been easy, and with budget cuts in many states, music programs have sometimes struggled to have the proper funding necessary to offer full, robust programs for their students. There have been wonderful, national fund-raising or philanthropic programs for music education such as the VH1 Save the Music Foundation or Barry Manilow's—Manilow Music Project—both dedicated to providing needed funds for school music programs.

Teaching can also be a part-time day job for the gigging musician, since in addition to classroom teaching or the aforementioned Internet sessions, some working musicians teach at music retail stores that offer on-site private lessons. Of course, private piano teachers have worked at home giving piano lessons for well over 100 years . . . making this form of music education the backbone of today's (and tomorrow's) leading keyboard players. And with lessons being offered on the Internet these days, if you don't want to spend time in the classroom each day, teaching lessons virtually through a private studio—or on your own—is yet another option.

Possibly, and most likely, you were in your school band, chorus, or orchestra when you were growing up. Therefore, you have a good sense of what the day-to-day tasks are for a classroom music teacher. But what does one have to know to be able to teach music? Certainly, first and foremost, you need to be an experienced and successful practitioner of the instrument(s) you're teaching. Demonstrate an accomplished level of musicianship: mastery of your instrument, conducting, sight-reading, singing, and studying a score. If you want to teach music in the public elementary, middle, or high school system, that will require a bachelor's degree in music and a teaching certificate.

Just as the music business has changed in many ways and many aspects in terms of how money is made in it, music for *religious services* has also changed in the last 25 years. Depending on with whom you're speaking, those changes have been either good or bad or both for church music today. But there's no denying that with the advent of praise bands, there are more opportunities these days for the gigging musician to make money making music in churches.

However, before you start eyeing that new guitar or electronic keyboard to be funded by the big bucks you'll rake in playing in churches, first know that most musicians in church worship bands are playing for the sheer joy of it. They are most often members of the church and are donating their time to the cause. That said, there are churches, synagogues, and cathedrals who pay musicians on a regular basis for their services (players and singers). And that's to say nothing of the full-time or part-time traditional or contemporary music director or worship leader. Add the usually paid, long-standing position of pianist and/or organist, and Sundays for working musicians can become not only a day to use your talents for a higher calling but a day to be paid for it as well (since the other regular gigs are generally closed that day). Many churches are happy and able to pay for worthwhile talent in order to enrich their services. Music is vital and integral to all church services and has been for centuries. Bach, Beethoven, Handel, and many other legendary classical musicians were church musicians, and their greatest works were commissioned and/or most often premiered and performed in churches. And that tradition continues to this day.

The broadest category of revenue streams presented in this chapter is *arts administration* (also known as *arts management*). If you're organized, artistically inclined, a good fund-raiser, and have a good sense of business and excellent people skills, arts administration could be a great match for you.

Symphonies, theatres, museums, opera houses, ballet companies . . . all of these types organizations fall under the category of arts organizations that are in need of management. These professional (usually nonprofit) entities are cultural enrichment centers in their respective communities. And they need personnel not only to manage them but to offer marketing and sales input and guidance, fund-raising expertise, ushers, ticket-takers, and more!

As with a music publisher or record label, depending on the size of an organization, you may or may not be asked to wear multiple hats. If you are in a small arts organization (a small to medium-sized symphony, for example), you may find yourself fund-raising in the morning, meeting with the orchestra conductor in the afternoon, and greeting patrons in the evening at a theatre event. Knowing how to write a grant for national, state, or local funding is crucial as well for leading players in the arts administration world.

As with the broader music business, so has the arts administration business changed due to the explosive growth of entertainment options available in the last 30 years. Competing for the entertainment dollar is a real challenge to any arts organization, regardless of size. So being aware of technology-based marketing programs (especially social media) is clearly important. Reaching out to younger patrons (especially children) is also a vital component of a growing a vibrant arts organization.

Finally, solid management techniques are a hallmark of superior arts management administrators. Managing a staff successfully—be it large or small—must be done to help the organization succeed in the midst of changing economic times.

When all of these elements are handled with success and focused passion, such organizations can be (and really should be) the cornerstone of musical and cultural activity of any community.

YOU CAN "MAKE IT RAIN!"

As you see from this chapter, the possibilities are there for a fulfilling living to "make it rain" and generate a living in the music business through a variety of revenue streams. And although this chapter covered all the major possibilities, there are still more to be had for those with creative ingenuity, ambition, and drive.

In the Mix: Money Management for Musicians

Money management and musicians don't always mix easily. One of the quickest pitfalls for independent artists and bands is to neglect the fundamentals of business and money management. Such areas don't always come easy to creative types (especially if you're being paid in cash for gigs, and that instant gratification makes it hard to resist spending instead of saving a portion). Here are seven key tips to assist in your financial protection . . . and survival.*

1. *You, Inc.* Consider forming an LLC (limited liability corporation) for your band or even if you're a solo artist. Such an entity protects your personal assets in the case of a lawsuit, and there are other benefits as well. Check out www.legalzoom.com for more information on the advantages of setting up different types of corporations. It's a good idea to separate your personal finances from those of the band, so you should open a separate bank account for the band. That will keep things "clean" and easy to track when it comes to tax time.

And make sure you plan cash flow carefully for the band. Have a regular time to pay everyone (including yourself), and anticipate expenses in advance compared to expected revenues. Make sure you won't run out of money!

2. *Feed the piggy (bank, that is).* The music business can be a roller coaster ride, full of big ups and downs. If you save money, you'll be able to pay rent and eat during the lean times. The key is to simply get into the habit of saving something . . . at least a little bit each week. Then when you're going on tour, making a recording, or the financial hard knocks happen (and they will), you're covered.

3. *Easy to Excel.* Spreadsheets can be intimidating for the uninitiated, but using Excel spreadsheet software (for example) to keep track of your income and expenses can spare you a lot of grief. Two of the most important words in any business are *comparative analysis*. With a spreadsheet, you can track your expenses versus revenues on a monthly and yearly basis. But more than just tracking them, you can compare last month's versus this month's . . . or any given month last year versus this year, and so forth. As you compare, you can determine where your band is going financially. Are you growing? Shrinking? Staying flat? This sort of analysis is invaluable so that you aren't surprised if there's less money in the till than expected in any given month. Spreadsheets also help you track financial trends in your career.

4. *Build a budget.* Band people and artists are naturally creative types, so the idea of coming up with a budget prior to getting out there and simply "making it happen" can be foreign to you. Whether you're preparing for a local gig at the Holiday Inn or a world tour . . . or recording a five-song EP, you need a budget! Sit down with a calculator in hand and your phone or laptop and write out all the anticipated expenses for the venture. Then, during the execution of the venture, you can keep checking back on your budget as the expenses occur to make sure you're on track. And if you're over budget halfway through the process, it's not too late to "trim your sails" and change direction by reducing expenses. Your EP can survive on four songs instead of five; your regional tour could lose a few cities to save on expenses.

5. *Dodge debt.* Debt is the ultimate enemy of any company (or band or artist). And while it's not always completely avoidable, it should be carefully considered and monitored. Sometimes you may need to borrow money from a bank to grow your business (and banks will lend provided you have enough collateral to back up the loan). But that can be a dark hole that's hard to climb out of in order to pay

back the loan on time and completely. Bottom line: plan finances carefully so as to stay out of debt.

6. *Juggle some balls.* Making money making music on a full-time basis isn't easy, at least not in one place. That is, if you're not teaching music (and even then, without a full-year salary, it can be a bit challenging). So think "laterally," not just "vertically." In other words, while you are building a career as a solo artist or in a band, think creatively to find other musical (or nonmusical) jobs to pay the rent. In addition to your work as a gigging musician, in a band, or as a solo artist, you might consider offering private lessons in singing, playing, and so on. Whatever it is you can do. Or you might work at a local arts organization such as a theatre or public arena. The Future of Music Coalition (www.futureofmusic.org) is a national nonprofit organization that has published a list of 40 revenue sources that musicians can draw upon.

7. *It's so taxing!* Self-employed musicians are like any other self-employed individuals: they are subject to paying their own taxes (vs. when an employer helps pay them for the employee). Tax laws change often, so it's a good idea to find a competent accountant to help you navigate the tricky tax waters. Make sure the accountant you choose comes highly recommended from a friend or associate.

*See also Dave Kusek, "5 Money Management Tips for Indie Musicians," *Sonicbids Blog*, May 1, 2014, http://blog.sonicbids.com/5-money-management-tips-for-indie-musicians.

NOTES

1. Espie Estrella, "The Role and Skills of a Music Arranger: Remixes, Remakes, and Fleshing Out Simple Music Ideas," ThoughtCo., February 26, 2018, https://www.thoughtco.com/the-music-arranger-2456200.

2. "Personal Manager," Get In Media, http://getinmedia.com/careers/personal-manager.

3. "What Does a Music Business Manager Do?" Sokanu, https://www.sokanu.com/careers/music-business-manager/.

4. "Entertainment Attorney," CareersinMusic.com, https://www.careersinmusic.com/entertainment-attorney/.

5. "Recording Engineer," CareersinMusic.com, https://www.careersinmusic.com/recording-engineer/.

6. Zannie Giraud Voss, Glenn B. Voss, and Karen Yair, *Orchestra Facts: 2006–2014* (New York: League of American Orchestras, 2016).

9

FROM BRICKS TO CLICKS

Retail and Merchandising

Don't try to explain it, just sell it.

—Colonel Tom Parker, manager of Elvis Presley

In today's digital age, one may ask: Are music retailers dinosaurs? The answer is a resounding no! That said, while digital delivery of music content has clearly had, and continues to have, a monumental impact on the physical "brick and mortar" retailing of music, the physical retailers that have embraced the digital age and used it to their advantage are not only surviving but, in many cases, thriving. More on some of those retailers later in this chapter—including the impact of digital retailers ("clicks").

The music products industry (guitars, keyboards, instruments, gear, and printed music) reported global retail sales of $16.0 billion in 2016.[1] That's actually a tiny component of the world's economy. It's less than the value of a day's worth of oil production, about 1/15 the value of global beer production, and smaller than about 450 individual companies. But musicians of the world, take heart! Everything is relative. Our work to have an impact on the world with the sounds and benefits of music have paid off and continue to do so. For example, 160 of the world's 196 nations are World Trade Organization members, and music products from the United States are exported to every one of them.[2] There's a huge trade imbalance when it comes to music and entertainment around the world, with the United States exporting far more to other parts of the world than it imports.[3] The world is hungry for the music and entertainment provided by the United States. And with many brick-and-mortar retailers now complementing their local store sales with online sales (which can reach around the world), international sales cannot be discounted. However, while it's good to get a perspective of music retail's global impact, what about the state of the neighborhood music store today?

TODAY'S BRICK-AND-MORTAR RETAILERS

In 2016, the music products industry in the United States generated $6.8 billion in new product revenues for retail stores and related websites.[4] These stores primarily serve amateur musicians in addition to professional musicians. Without amateur/hobbyist musicians, the music retail business would be out of business. The retail industry also includes services such as instrument repair and lessons, rounding out music retail revenues to still-impressive numbers.

Job opportunities abound in music retail stores (physical or online) either as an employee or a proprietor. This is particularly true for students or others seeking part-time or seasonal employment. There are different types of music retail stores, but the primary types are full-line stores, combo stores, school music stores, and specialty shops.

Full-line retail stores carry everything from pianos, drums, guitars, band instruments, organs, orchestra, percussion, and printed music, as well as aforementioned services such as instrument repair and lessons. According to *Musical Merchandise Review*, one of the leading trade magazines in the music products industry, there are 7,650 full-line music stores currently in the United States at this writing. The largest retailers in this category are Guitar Center, Sweetwater, Sam Ash, Schmitt Music, Brook Mays, and Quinlan & Fabish Music.[5] These stores' revenues annually number in the millions of dollars. These music store equivalents of a Walmart or Home Depot have challenged independent music ("mom and pop") retailers in the past (and often won), but some independent stores still survive and thrive.

Combo stores don't carry the full spectrum of music products but instead focus on drums, guitars, gear, and accessories.

School music stores cater to the educational market, specializing in serving schools and colleges/universities. School band and orchestra directors, as well as private piano teachers, often rely on these stores for music and equipment. Parents often rent, rent-to-own, or outright purchase instruments for their children from these stores, which can be a lucrative business. Instrumental repair services walk hand in hand with this line of business for the school music store.

Fig 9.1.   Premiere Music Retailer Guitar Center

Specialty shops are geared to more advanced and professional musicians, and while they carry a more limited range of products (such as guitars, drums, and sound equipment), the depth of products they carry within that line is deeper. For example, the famous Gruhn Guitars is a specialty musical instrument shop in Nashville. Its product line is narrow, in that it specializes in guitars. From vintage guitars to new ones from factories and independent manufacturers, it's a mecca for rock and country stars and wealthy collectors. Gruhn's customer base boasts the likes of Duane Allman, Mark Knopfler, Conan O'Brien, Robert Plant, and Eric Clapton.[6]

Another common specialty store is the *piano store*, which sells . . . you guessed it, pianos! From simple studio uprights to baby and full grand pianos . . . some acoustic only; others fully equipped with digital mechanisms to play recorded performances by activating the piano hammers . . . this store is a piano player's paradise.

A 2015 article from the *Guardian* reported that in the United States, piano stores have been closing "as kids snub lessons for other activities" such as amateur sports and newer computer-oriented activities.[7] Another challenge for piano stores selling new pianos is the abundance of piano technicians who can repair quality used pianos and sell them at a much lower cost than new ones.

Additionally, in a 2015 article by an AXS contributor, it was reported that some historic Detroit piano stores were closing.[8] The article went on:

"Detroit used to have dozens and dozens of piano sellers back in the early 20th century and in 1909, more than 364,500 pianos were sold. In fact, in the city's heyday, it was one of the largest sellers of the instrument. But these days, many of the old retailers have closed down. As for recent sales? Between 30,000 and 40,000 . . . a massive decline."[9]

Another factor in the declining sales of pianos in the United States is that pianos last a long time; high-quality, properly-maintained pianos can remain playable for 60 to 80 years after their original purchase. The high price of pianos is one factor that is causing the closing of piano stores: A good grand piano from a respected name costs about as much as a luxury automobile, and as such, children (and their parents) are choosing less expensive instruments, such as electronic keyboards or stringed instruments.

"However, in China, piano sales are booming, with most of these piano sales being intended for home use; this rise in sales is in part because the costly instruments are viewed as a status symbol in China."[10]

Another specialty shop features violins. Despite having a variety of different stringed instruments, these so-called violin shops are often operated by luthiers (violinmakers) who make violin family instruments and bows for sale. These luthiers also do repairs and maintenance on such instruments.

WHAT'S SELLING?

What are the most popular items in music retail stores overall? The National Association of Music Merchants (NAMM) is the leading trade association of music retailers. According to NAMM, here are the best-selling product categories in their member stores:

1. Fretted products (primarily guitars)
2. Sound reinforcement products
3. Wind instruments
4. Printed music
5. General accessories
6. Microphones
7. Percussion
8. Computer music products
9. Acoustic pianos
10. Signal processing
11. Instrument amplifiers
12. Portable keyboards[11]

NAMM holds significant trade shows during each year (winter and summer) to showcase the latest musical instruments, professional audio equipment, music electronics, software, and printed music. NAMM also provides educational seminars at these trade shows designed to help music retailers grow and improve their sales.

The top four best-selling product categories deserve to be examined a bit, since prospective employees or owners of music retail stores should be well versed in these areas.

Guitars. Fretted instruments, particularly guitars, are the most popular items sold in music retail stores. Emerging first in the 1930s, electric guitars are among the most popular musical instruments in music stores. Electric guitars can be heard in a variety of music types—from pop rock, blues, jazz, heavy metal, and funk to hip-hop. Best-known brands include Gibson, Fender, and Ibanez. In addition to selling guitars, stores that stock them also carry a wide variety of guitar accessories (picks, straps, cases, etc.).[12]

Sound reinforcement systems. These often-complicated systems contain a combination of microphones, signal processors, amplifiers, and loudspeakers that are all controlled by a mixing board that makes live or prerecorded sounds louder. Sound reinforcement systems are used everywherre from schools to churches to athletic stadiums and arenas. The systems found in major stadiums and arenas are typically more complex than others as they often contain hundreds of microphones, complex sound-mixing and signal-processing systems, multiple speaker configurations, and so forth. But sound systems can also be as simple as a single microphone connected to a 100-watt amplifier for a singer at a local music club.[13]

Wind instruments. This segment of the music retail business is healthy and encompasses selling (or renting or renting-to-own) everything from trumpets and trombones to song flutes and saxophones. The National Association of School Music Dealers (NASMD) is the association of retail stores in the United States that cater to this market, mostly consisting of band and orchestra teachers and their students.

Printed music. Although one might think that with the advent of the digital age printed music seems like a "horse and buggy" operation, the truth is quite the opposite. Today's leading print music publishers (Hal Leonard Corporation and Alfred Music, as mentioned in chapter 6) are cutting-edge companies that not only still produce physical products but offer digital downloads as well. The world's largest retailer of print music is privately owned J. W. Pepper, based in Exton, Pennsylvania, with retail stores coast to coast. Founded in 1876 by James Walsh Pepper, the company has remained on the cutting edge of print music retailing while expanding into companion areas such as music accessories. Pepper has led the way in the electronic delivery of sheet music ("Pepper e-Print") for school and church directors, students, and hobbyists.

A full-line music retail store stocks pop folios, piano music, band, orchestra and choral music . . . all covering the full range of music styles.

OTHER SINGLE-CATEGORY STORES

Pro audio. Not only do pro audio stores obviously sell high-end audio products, they also sell and rent a variety of sound system components, Public Address (PA) systems, musical gear, stage pianos, and bass amps.

Used music stores. These music stores are found in practically every major and minor U.S. city. From used records, cassettes, and CDs to vintage instruments, printed music, and sound gear, used music stores offer discount prices for collectibles and more.

ONLINE MUSIC RETAILERS/
DIGITAL MUSIC DELIVERY

From bricks to clicks . . . the business of selling music products online has exploded in the last decade. This form of selling music products shows no signs of slowing down. It has clearly had an impact on the physical store, but most (if not all) physical music retail stores at least have a website, if not e-commerce on their website to sell physical products.

The *online music retail store* sells music files over the Internet. From audio files to downloadable PDF files of printed music, this segment of the music retail business has continued to have a strong presence. The world's largest online digital music retailer is Apple's iTunes.[14] The online music retail store offers the ability to purchase and download files, while a streaming service is offered through a subscription. A subscription service (such as Spotify) does not offer downloads for sale.

JOB AND CAREER OPPORTUNITIES

Opportunities and types of positions available in music retail stores are varied, depending on whether you are considering an independent music retailer versus a national chain. Jobs also vary according to the size of store.

But in general, here are the positions that are present in today's music retailers (in addition to president and/or owner, of course):

- General manager
- Sales associate (and/or front-counter clerk)
- Marketing/webmaster
- Specialty buyer (piano, orchestral instruments, print music, etc.)
- Instructor (piano, guitar, instrumental, voice)
- Accounting
- Inventory/warehouse
- Shipping

THE FUTURE OF MUSIC RETAIL

It's anyone's guess as to what the future holds for bricks versus clicks in the music retail business in years to come. But if the most recent past is any indicator, its future is bright and will be a hybrid where content is king and those retailers who offer the easiest and most economical manner of obtaining that content will be the winners. Yet the numbers, history, and statistics of the music retail business can't tell the full story or reflect the passion and hard work of the people who make it all happen decade after decade, one customer at a time . . . and the emotional fulfillment they help bring about through making music.

NOTES

1. Paul A. Majeski, "The Annual Census of the Music Industries," *Music Trades* magazine, www.musictrades.com.

2. Majeski, "Annual Census."

3. Bureau of Economic Analysis, *U.S. International Trade in Goods and Services Report, January 2018* (Washington, DC: U.S. Census Bureau, 2018).

4. Majeski, "Annual Census."

5. *Musical Merchandise Review* Supplier Directory, http://www.mmrmagazine .com/directory.

6. "Gruhn Guitars," Wikipedia, https://en.wikipedia.org/wiki/Gruhn_Guitars.

7. "Piano Stores Closing across US as Kids Snub Lessons for Other Activities," *Guardian*, January 2, 2015, https://www.theguardian.com/us-news/2015/jan/02/ piano-stores-closing-kids-snub-lessons-compete-technology.

8. Michael Ferro, "Detroit Piano Stores Closing amid Country's Lack of Interest in Ebony and Ivory," AXS, January 5, 2015, www.axs.com/detroit-piano-stores -closing-amid-country-s-lack-of-interest-in-ebony--35842.

9. Ferro, "Detroit Piano Stores Closing."

10. Thibaud (blog), "The Piano Industry in China: A Musical Trend," Daxue Consulting, March 21, 2016, http://daxueconsulting.com/the-piano-industry-in -china/.

11. National Association of Music Merchants, "Industry," NAMM University, https://www.namm.org/nammu/industry.

12. "Music Store," Wikipedia, https://en.wikipedia.org/wiki/Music_store.

13. "Sound Reinforcement System," Wikipedia, https://en.wikipedia.org/ wiki/Sound_reinforcement_system.

14. NPD Group, "The NPD Group—After 10 Years Apple Continues Music Download Dominance in the U.S.," press release, NPD.com, April 2017, https:// www.npd.com/wps/portal/npd/us/news/press-releases/the-npd-group-after10 -years-apple-continues-music-download-dominance-in-the-u-s/.

10

WHERE HOLLYWOOD
MEETS BROADWAY

Music for Broadcasting, Film, and Theatre

> To me, movies and music go hand in hand. When I'm writ-
> ing a script, one of the first things I do is find the music I'm
> going to play for the opening sequence.
>
> —Quentin Tarantino

Of all the parts of the music business, Hollywood and Broadway offer a uniquely high level of excitement and "sizzle." The mediums of film and broadcasting can potentially offer an unprecedented platform for one's music and for those who facilitate getting the music out through those conduits. And while Broadway performances are limited to how many people a theatre can seat on the famous Great White Way, a hit musical can rack up hundreds (if not thousands) of performances, garnering massive box office receipts along with the substantial money generated from a hit show in a variety of other mediums—such as recordings, broadcasting, and film—to say nothing of touring companies. Put it all together and you see there is a world of unlimited opportunities in making music for film, broadcasting, and theatre.

That said, before you book your plane ticket to fame and fortune, let me hasten to add this area of the music business is arguably even more competitive and brutal than other parts, due to the high-profile nature of it and the potential rewards. But that shouldn't daunt anyone who truly wants to make a living in this segment of the business and is singularly focused on making it happen . . . for that is what it takes to make it in this highly competitive area.

The good news: Since a large portion of the music business requires music to be written for these mediums—television in particular—they are extremely hungry for content, therefore offering excellent creative and monetary opportunities for composers, arrangers, orchestrators, producers, number crunchers, and more. More good news is that you needn't have the talent of legendary award-winning film and television composer John Williams to participate (but it certainly wouldn't hurt!). And as with all the wheels of the music business, the recording and publishing industries often interact with film, television, and theatre . . . making it necessary and highly desirable to have a fundamental understanding of how this side of the business works and the opportunities that abound in this exciting world.

LIGHTS, CAMERA . . . MUSIC!

Most uses of music in television and film have similar rules and personnel to make it all happen. Let's first consider broadcasting (television and radio, as well as other media) in its use of music.

MUSIC IN BROADCASTING

Broadcasting has experienced broad changes in the last few decades and continues to evolve. Prior to the invention of recording technology (and television), all music broadcast on radio was "live." Imagine that world . . . where any time that music was used there had to be live musicians performing it. When the possibility of recording music came to be, everything changed, and although it obviously greatly reduced the possibility of live gigs for musicians performing on radio, it enormously increased the need for new technologies, recording engineers, arrangers, producers, composers, and so forth. The modern broadcast era for the music business was born. With great change comes great opportunity.

Today's world of television has undergone, and is continuing to undergo, sweeping changes as the 18–49 aged demographic evolves in how they consume entertainment. The 18–49 demographic continues to be the most attractive to advertisers since they are convinced the 50-plus crowd's minds are pretty made up in terms of their buying habits. In the "old days," when there were only the "Big Three" television networks (as they were called in the 1960s and 1970s: ABC, CBS, NBC), the landscape was very different, with only three channel choices. With the advent of cable television and hundreds of channels, plus the Internet, and then on-demand services such as Netflix, Hulu, Sling TV, and so forth, the future of traditional broadcast television is open for discussion, as is what role broadcast networks will play on the entertainment landscape in the long-term future. Add in the fact that the device that is used to view content has changed, and that "thickens the plot" as well. Seldom do today's children sit in front of a traditional television set. They're more likely using a handheld device to view their favorite content as it streams on YouTube or is downloaded from iTunes or Amazon. But as stated before, with change comes opportunity. With this proliferation of media outlets comes numerous ways to plug in to using your talents, since—due to so many media outlet choices—the demand for programming (which contains music content, either as featured or underscore) has obviously grown. Still, despite those opportunities, it's initially difficult for production companies to turn a profit on shows they produce due to enormous production costs. It's on the "back end" (future local television syndication, cable, foreign sales, home video distribution, Internet streaming and downloads, etc.) where a show can be profitable. But ultimately, profitable they can be and sometimes wildly profitable. And those profits create possibilities for people in the music business.

So where is music used on television? Most of these you already know as a consumer, but when putting a list together, it's an eye-opener as to how much the medium relies on music for content:

- Theme songs *(some shows still use them)*
- Background music *(music used to complement the mood of what's happening visually, usually with spoken dialogue over it)*
- Music underscore *(music used to match and heighten the mood of what's happening visually, sometimes with no dialogue over it)*
- Music specials/awards shows *(this format has enjoyed excellent growth over the years)*
- Music videos *(very important, now more than ever with the arrival of YouTube)*
- News, sports, special-event programming *(on the local and national levels)*

All of the above use new, original music and/or existing music. As the old saying goes, "Everything is negotiable." But as a rule of thumb, for original music most television contracts require the music composed to be as work for hire, for which the program producer becomes the copyright owner. There are exceptions to this rule (depending on who's doing the composing, for example), but in general composers of original music can expect to sign the copyright over to the program producer. Of course, for existing music that already has recognition and popularity, the original publisher of the song retains the copyright.

Rates vary as to what a production company pays to a composer and/or music publisher depending on the use. For example, a theme song earns considerably more than background music. A "featured song" in a television show—where the actor sings or plays the song and no dialogue is spoken over it—will garner more money than a song that is used as background music. Fragments of songs earn less than when a full song is used, and so on.

For film, broadcasting, and other media, there are also various music production libraries that offer royalty-free "stock" music for a fee to program producers. These production libraries have vast music themes, "cues" (short motifs to underscore, connect, or begin/end scenes), background, foreground, and other music to serve television (and radio and film and other media). Often the music is not only owned but produced by these companies.

Next, who's making it happen? Here's a list of the prominent music-related roles in television and film. Imagine yourself possibly taking on one of these positions:

1. *Film composer.* These talented people work collaboratively with directors, producers, writers, and even the actors occasionally. The composer sits with the producer, director, film editor, and music editor in a "spotting session." The director and composer watch the film and "spot" it—identifying where and what type of music should and shouldn't be used. This is based on a number of factors such as the emotional content of the film, what type of music will support the scene, and so forth.

2. *Music supervisor.* Akin to a record producer, A&R (artist and repertoire) person, or music publisher, this is the person who, by the broadest definition, curates then combines music and visual media. According to the Guild of Music Supervisors, a music supervisor is "a qualified professional who oversees all music-related aspects of film, television, advertising, video games, and other existing or emerging visual media platforms as required."[1] In the musical theatre industry, a music supervisor manages a team of music directors working on different aspects of the production. (More on musical theatre later.)

3. *Clearance representative.* This individual is responsible for procuring licenses for (or "clearing") copyrighted material from outside publishers for use. Clearance representatives are often part of a company that is separate from a producer, although major televi-

sion and film companies often have an in-house clearance person or staff.

4. *Music director.* This position is rare but still exists in television today when a leader of an on-air band is used. Network television shows such as *The Tonight Show* (NBC) or *The Late Show* (CBS) employ a music director (or more simply, "bandleader"). In radio, the station's music director chooses songs for airplay.

5. *Orchestra musicians.* These session players are usually American Federation of Musicians (AFM) members, and in Hollywood, New York, and Nashville, they are the cream of the crop. They are able to sight-read most any score and be ready to record it after one read-through (or even record it on the first take if need be). These players also often have jobs in the local symphony orchestra, but in the major recording centers, the recording business is so robust there is no time for these top-tier players to do anything other than studio recording.

TRADITIONAL AND NONTRADITIONAL BROADCAST OUTLETS

While this chapter section has focused primarily on television, radio also has its many uses for music content. In the earlier days of radio, it was transmitted exclusively "on the air" through use of transmission towers for either AM (amplitude modulation) or FM (frequency modulation) signals. Those "terrestrial" days of radio still exist, but satellite radio services, such as SiriusXM, have replaced many listeners' desire for traditional terrestrial radio. Add to the mix Internet streaming radio platforms such as iHeart Radio (called *webcasting*) and the reach of radio as we once knew it has been increased greatly. Though the death of radio has been predicted for years, it still remains a very viable medium and an outlet for volumes of music content.

Music videos most certainly play an integral part in the music business. Music videos use existing songs that are released either simultaneously with the song or soon after the song's initial release. Few would realize music videos have their roots reaching back to 1894, when music print publishers Edward B. Marks and Joe Stern promoted sales of their song "The Little Lost Child." Marks and Stern hired electrician George Thomas and various performers. Thomas used a magic lantern (an early type of image projector) to project a series of still images on a screen synchronized to live performances.

This form of entertainment was known as the illustrated song, the forerunner of the modern music video.[2] Little did Marks and Stern know how powerful music videos would eventually become in the marketing of songs.

When a music video is made for a song (which is most of the time), the record company typically charges 50 percent of the cost of the video production against the artist's audio royalty and 100 percent against an artist's video royalty. The reason the chargeback is only 50 percent for the cost of the artist's audio recording is that the recording was made by the record company prior to the video being produced. Therefore, the recording expense needn't be recouped as a part of the video expense.

The largest purveyor of music videos in today's Internet age is YouTube.[3] Although YouTube isn't a traditional broadcast outlet, its impact on the music business has arguably become much more of a factor in the launching and consumption of music nowadays than all of the current broadcast networks combined.

YouTube is a video-sharing website based in San Bruno, California. Three former PayPal employees founded the site in 2005. Google purchased YouTube in November 2006 for $1.6 billion. Most of the content on YouTube is uploaded by individuals, but media corporations such as CBS, BBC, and Hulu can be easily found on the site. All types of music genres are found on YouTube.[4]

YouTube has become larger than iTunes and other Internet sources for the consumption of music and music videos . . . covering all genres of music from rock and pop to classical, sacred, and much more.

In addition to YouTube, Vevo (an abbreviation for "video evolution") is a video-hosting service founded in 2009 as a joint venture among the Big Three record companies (Universal, Sony, and Warner Music Group).[5]

MUSIC IN FILM

It has been said the best film score is one the audience doesn't notice. It's so organically meshed with the film's images that it never intrudes on the visuals and doesn't call attention to itself but flows seamlessly with the film. Then there are those musical moments in film that become as memorable as the film itself. The two-note motif for the shark in *Jaws* is one of the most glaring examples. Music used in film is a powerful tool, and when used artfully, it can become an indelible (if not life-changing) experience.

Scoring music for films doesn't only take place in Hollywood, of course. There are numerous opportunities in major cities to write film scores for independent ("indie") films. These are especially good options for the beginning film composer, who can learn not only how to apply his or her talents for writing a successful score but also to do so with less than a big-budget picture, which often spurs even more creativity.

Most would-be film composers get their start by writing for smaller projects (commercials, local television, etc.). By building a network of connections in the film music community, this can lead to assisting a successful film composer through an apprenticeship. Also, many universities such as the University of California, Los Angeles; University of Southern California; Berklee College of Music; Belmont University; and New York University have first-rate film scoring programs, arguably the best way to get a start in writing music for film and television.

Similar to television programs, there are three primary types of music used in film: the underscore, the original song written for the film, and the previously existing song. Also similar to television, different uses are remunerated accordingly based on the value and placement of the music used. Many other factors come into play, such as the film's overall budget, the duration of the use, the frequency of use, whether there is a change in the original lyrics (for a previously existing song), whether there's a guarantee the song will be used on the film's soundtrack, and so on.

Music cue sheets play a vital role in film music remuneration. Such a sheet is prepared by the film's producer after the film has been finished. The sheet lists all the music used in the motion picture, including:

- How each song was used (featured, background, underscore, etc.)
- Length of each use
- Writer credits
- Publisher credits
- PRO (performing rights organization) affiliation of each song
- If the original master recording was used (which would have required a master usage license)
- Recording artist name(s)
- Record company name(s) (if original masters were used)
- Scene and dialogue details

Since ASCAP, BMI, and SESAC rely on these cue sheets to know whom to pay for the respective uses, publishers and writers are often advised to review the sheets along with the PROs to make sure all information is accurate.

FOLLOW THE GREEN . . . UH, *YELLOW* BRICK ROAD

Once again, as is the case with a television program after its initial release, movies often make the most money after their initial theatrical release. As for a song featured in a movie, here's the path of potential additional monetization for a successful song (such as "My Heart Will Go On" from *Titanic*):

1. Broadcast performance of the song on television and radio
2. Soundtrack recordings (CD/DVD/Blu-ray) and downloads
3. Streaming services
4. Awards shows (if nominated; e.g., Grammys, Golden Globes, Academy Awards)
5. Print music
6. Eventual television broadcast airings (of the film)
7. Pay TV, cable TV, streaming video
8. Commercial (if allowed by writer/publisher to advertise a product)
9. Ringtones
10. Video games
11. International sales
12. Miscellaneous royalties (unique uses, such as greeting cards or dolls that contain music-playing computer chips)

The above uses for a hit song in a film can yield millions of dollars initially and many more millions in the years to come. Another perfect example of such revenues is "Over the Rainbow" from *The Wizard of Oz*, which has earned billions in total revenues since its 1939 release. The obvious sum total is that if a writer or publisher lands a hit song in a film (or a writer composes a complete score for a movie), the monetary rewards are potentially staggering, providing a lifetime revenue stream for writer and publisher alike.

MUSIC IN THEATRE

Musical theatre is a uniquely American popular art form. The beginning of musical theatre reaches back to a show titled *The Black Crook*, premiering in New York City on September 12, 1866. But American musical theatre's roots are firmly grounded in European operetta traditions and Edwardian musical comedy. Groundbreaking American musicals such as Kern and Hammerstein's *Show Boat* (1927) and Rodgers and Hammerstein's *Oklahoma!* (1943) integrated music and book for the first time, stretching the previous purely light entertainment form of musicals. These shows paved the way for iconic musicals to follow, such as Meredith Willson's *The Music Man* (1957), *West Side Story* (1957), *Hair* (1967), *A Chorus Line* (1975), *The Phantom of the Opera* (1986), *Rent* (1996), and *Hamilton* (2015).[6]

The two major theatre performance areas in New York City are Broadway and Off-Broadway. The Broadway Theatre (simply referred to as "Broadway"), includes professional theatres "with 500 or more seats located in the Theater District and Lincoln Center along Broadway in Midtown Manhattan." The Theater District is a very popular tourist-attraction area in New York. "Along with London's West End theatre, Broadway theatre is considered to be the highest level of commercial theatre in the English-speaking world."[7]

Off-Broadway theatres seat between 100 and 499 and are scattered throughout Manhattan. Off-Broadway is often a launching pad for Broadway shows, provided the content can appeal to a wide-enough audience to support the costs of mounting a Broadway show.[8]

Some Off-Broadway musicals are never transferred to Broadway simply because the larger venue could eclipse the show, making it lose its original charm. This has certainly happened through the years to various Off-Broadway shows, and the transfer is always regretted by all involved.

Successful shows often tour throughout the United States, with megasuccessful shows mounting productions around the world, such as *The Phantom of the Opera* and *The Lion King*. Broadway musicals can also be found in Las Vegas, on cruise ships, or even in abbreviated versions in theme parks.

Therefore, once again, if the "needle" is threaded correctly when writing a musical that becomes supersuccessful, the financial rewards for the creative team and producers are astronomical. Now for the bad news: Most musicals lose money for their investors on Broadway, and far more miss rather than hit. But if the musical makes it to Broadway, even if its "run" (the length of consecutive performances given) is short, the producers may opt to take it on the road, since having had a Broadway run gives it instant credibility around the nation. Plus, a show panned by the New York critics may often play very well in other parts of the country.

Rights that are granted for the performance of musicals are grand rights and small rights. *Grand rights* is a term that refers to the rights contained in the context of a dramatic work such as a musical or concert dance. Grand rights fall into the intellectual property rights category. (See chapter 3 for more details on intellectual property rights.) While Section 115 of U.S. copyright law provides that a compulsory license be offered to perform copyrighted musical compositions, as administered by PROs, the provision's scope only applies to nondramatic performances. As such, the license agreements of major PROs such as ASCAP and BMI only cover what are known in contrast as "small rights" and exclude the use of compositions within "dramatic" or "dramatico-musical" works or the use of compositions that originated from a dramatico-musical work. Unlike small rights, grand rights must be negotiated directly with the publisher or copyright holder of the composition.

If the show has at least been moderately successful on Broadway or Off-Broadway, an original cast recording (OCR) is made. These recordings become a permanent record of the show. While in the early days of Broadway musicals such cast recordings sold millions of copies, nowadays cast recordings don't sell as robustly as they once did.

After creating a show, and once it has been performed (on Broadway, Off-Broadway, or regionally), the show is usually licensed for additional productions coast to coast and possibly worldwide. These rights are generally assigned to theatrical licensing houses, such as Music Theatre International (MTI), Tams-Witmark, Rodgers and Hammerstein, and so on. Shows can only be licensed exclusively by one organization (akin to a songwriter only belonging to one PRO). The licensing agency grants a license to theatres wishing to produce the show and then collects a royalty for this license for all performances. These performances, over a period of decades if the show was very successful on Broadway, also serve as a major revenue stream for the writers and certain creative team members of the show.

Here are the major team members in the creation of a Broadway musical:

- Producer
- General manager
- Stage manager
- House manager
- Dance captain
- Casting director
- Advertising

- Press representative
- Actors

The creative team consists of:

- Composer and lyricist
- Librettist
- Director
- Choreographer
- Set designer
- Costume designer
- Lighting designer
- Musical director
- Sound designer
- Orchestrator
- Dance arranger

This doesn't include the other support staff members needed to keep a show up and running, such as:

- Backstage dressers (those who help actors with fast costume changes)
- Carpenter and master carpenter
- Electrician
- Front of house (ushers/box office)
- Master electrician
- Paint crew
- Playbill writer (the playbill is the printed program for the show)
- Publicist
- Scenic artist
- Theatrical technician
- Technical director
- Stagehands
- Wardrobe supervisor

Therefore, there are a lot of possibilities worth exploring when working for a musical.

Entering the theatrical field is best started locally . . . in community theatres, nearby repertory companies, and school/college productions. These venues provide needed experience to work one's way up to larger theatres and, if so desired, the grandest platform, as considered by most: Broadway.

The broadcast, film, and theatre industries offer potentially exciting and very rewarding careers for all sorts of disciplines from the music business world. As Irving Berlin wrote, "There's no business like show business!"

NOTES

1. Guild of Music Supervisors website, http://www.guildofmusicsupervisors .com.

2. Jack Pattenden, "January 1, 1894: The Illustrated Song," *The History of the Music Video*, TimeToast.com, https://www.timetoast.com/timelines/the-history-of -the-music-video--6.

3. Peter Kafka, "YouTube, the World's Biggest Music Service, Finally Launches Its Own Music Service," Recode, November 12, 2015, https://www .recode.net/2015/11/12/11620608/youtube-the-worlds-biggest-music-service -finally-launches-its-own.

4. "YouTube," Wikipedia, https://en.wikipedia.org/wiki/YouTube.

5. "Vevo," Wikipedia, https://en.wikipedia.org/wiki/Vevo.

6. "Musical Theatre," Wikipedia, https://en.wikipedia.org/wiki/Musical_the- atre.

7. "Broadway Theatre," Wikipedia, https://en.wikipedia.org/wiki/Broadway_ theatre.

8. "Off-Broadway," Wikipedia, https://en.wikipedia.org/wiki/Off-Broadway.

11

BEETHOVEN ON MAIN STREET

Arts Administration

> The arts are the one thing that appeal right across all forms of
> politics, race, creed—everything.
>
> —Andrew Lloyd Webber

As has been a theme in this book, the music business can be a deeply
rewarding and exciting career but is often difficult to break into. Yet
there are so many areas that it encompasses (and accordingly so many types
of jobs), that if you have a passion for it (with the matching skills and de-
termination), there's a place waiting for you!

In my estimation, no book on the music business is complete unless
it includes the exciting and vital area of *arts administration* (or *arts management*). While this area might not have the "sizzle" some see with other areas
such as touring, recording, publishing, or artist management, if a person
is matched to arts administration's particular challenges and rewards, it is
equally as profitable and exhilarating as other areas.

The arts is obviously a very broad term that encompasses a wide range
of artistic disciplines: music, theatre, art, dance, and literature. Arts administration therefore encompasses the administration of all of those disciplines
through various organizations . . . another one of its major appeals, especially to those who enjoy variety.

On the music side of things, arts administration generally centers
around classical or so-called serious music (symphony orchestras, opera,
ballet, community concert associations). Such organizations are generally
nonprofit. That's not to say that plenty of arts administration jobs aren't
found in the for-profit sector (local performing arts centers or certain museums, for example).

Fig 11.1.   Lincoln Center

Business operations are ultimately at the heart of all arts administration jobs, with the head of an arts organization facilitating day-to-day operations of that organization. Such organizations can be large symphony orchestras or smaller music organizations such as a chamber choir. The duties of an arts administrator can include staff management, marketing, budget management, public relations, fund-raising, program development and evaluation, and board relations (since most such organizations have local governing boards). If you enjoy being "behind the scenes" (as well as occasionally having to be out front) making exciting artistic events for the community happen, this world offers that and more. Accordingly, the role of an arts administrator is varied and potentially very exciting, challenging, and rewarding . . . and at the same time has a deep impact on individuals and a community at large. More specifics on that role later.

Nearly all cities in the United States have performing arts facilities of one form or another, whether as a part of a local public or private high school or college or as a civically funded entity. Two of the top centers for the performing arts in the United States are Lincoln Center (New York City) and the John F. Kennedy Center for the Performing Arts (Washington, DC).

A BIT OF ARTS HISTORY

During the 1960s, the arts in the United States experienced an exciting period of growth and change. Experimental art forms such as pop art and poetry "happenings" (public poetry readings) took place. The then still relatively new medium of television offered mass exposure to artistic events as never before, drawing new public attention to the arts. As television ownership grew, so did arts exposure. Suddenly, art events in various major cities across the United States were seen nationally. This new attention, in turn, brought larger audiences to theatres, museums, and performances than in previous decades.[1]

For example, the Young People's Concerts at the New York Philharmonic in Lincoln Center is the longest-running series of family concerts of classical music in the world. The concerts were hosted by famed New York Philharmonic conductor and composer Leonard Bernstein. Beginning in 1962, the concerts were broadcast on the CBS television network from Lincoln Center.[2]

Furthermore, art growth in America was fueled even more by the civil rights and women's movements. As growing numbers of African Americans and women were allowed to participate in professional artistic performance and production, fresh insights were added to the mix. Add to this the growing overall commercialism in modern American society of that era and the sum total was an explosion of the arts.[3]

This growth and exposure fueled television viewing of the arts, in particular through the Public Broadcasting Service (PBS) and the Corporation for Public Broadcasting (CPB). Additionally, a number of new arts-oriented cable channels eventually sprang up, such as the Arts and Entertainment Network (A&E) and Bravo. National Public Radio (NPR) also continues to be a source of arts, entertainment, and informational programming.

CLASSICAL MUSIC

The classical music field intersects largely with the area of arts administration, since the above-mentioned outlets and funding often benefit classical music most and vice versa. On the "flip side," however, only a relatively small portion of the music-consuming public has a concentrated interest in classical music. According to the 2015 Nielsen Music Report, the most recent statistics of recorded sales put classical music at 2 percent of overall recorded music sales (which includes CDs, vinyl, downloads, and streaming).[4] Still, that's a significant amount when you consider the global recording industry is a multibillion-dollar enterprise. Leading classical music labels such as Deutsche Grammophon and Naxos have forged a substantial niche for themselves, becoming very successful in this genre.

In addition to traditional classical recordings of Beethoven, Bach, Mozart, and others, there have been artists who have been successful at *crossing over* from the classical world to pop listeners (with classical music or neoclassical music). Artists such as Jackie Evancho, Josh Groban, Andrea Bocelli, and others have crossed over from classical to mainstream.

The symphony orchestra world is a mainstay of arts administration. This area offers a healthy set of opportunities for classically trained musicians and those who are in the management side of things as well. The official organization for symphony orchestras, the League of American Orchestras, is a nonprofit service and educational organization dedicated to strengthening symphony and chamber orchestras. Its annual convention draws delegates from throughout the country.

Of all the symphony orchestras in the United States, about 50 of them boast a budget of $1 million or much more.[5] The result is thousands of jobs cumulatively for music business job seekers. Many symphony orchestras also have volunteer, semiprofessional, or professional choral groups associated with them, therefore increasing the possibility of employment and involvement.

THE ROLE OF THE ARTS ADMINISTRATOR

So what does it take to be an arts administrator in a large or small organization? Here are some of the main skills and personal qualities needed:

- an interest in the arts in general, or a particular art form;
- administrative and computer skills;
- good written and spoken communication skills;
- the ability to organize and prioritize work;
- problem-solving skills;
- good time-management skills;
- the ability to meet deadlines and keep calm under pressure;
- commercial awareness; and
- the ability to make information accessible to a wide range of people.

ISSUES IN ARTS ADMINISTRATION

As with most any business, arts organizations are also susceptible to local, regional, and national changes and trends. External changes may be cultural, social, demographic, economic, political, legal, or technological. Internal changes may be related to the audience, membership, board of directors, personnel, facilities, growth, or financial operations. Another change that must be taken into consideration is the growing need for technology-based marketing programs (i.e., social media) in order for the organization to change with the times and bring younger visitors and member pools into the organization.

Although a good arts administrator constantly monitors and manages change, he or she must also remain aware of the overall direction and mood of the organization while helping people do their day-to-day jobs.

FUNDING

Arts organizations, as part of the economic system, experience the effects of expansion and contractions in the local, regional, national, and world economies. Many arts organizations struggle in difficult economic times. Even in booming economic times, funding is always at the top of the "to do" list of any arts center. Even a well-known performing arts center such as the Kennedy Center in Washington, DC, has to be in tune with funding needs and have programs and plans in place to not only survive but thrive. Therefore, a variety of fresh programs and ideas help keep people interested, engaged, attending . . . and donating! Most arts organizations have a subscription series of some type, wherein patrons can purchase reduced-price tickets for concerts by committing to buying a ticket(s) to an entire season of concerts. These subscription series often come with additional perks such as preferred seating and free valet parking.

VENUE MANAGEMENT

A close cousin of the role of arts administrator is that of *concert venue manager*. Venue manager is not as broad a job as arts administrator. This person takes care of booking the venue, interacting with a variety of clients . . . from Broadway touring companies to local dance studios (depending on the size and scope of the venue). The concert venue manager also negotiates hiring fees and works with the venue's artistic director or program planner. In addition, the venue manager assures the venue's profitability and the artistic quality of the venue's offerings and meets the needs of community groups.

Other duties may include budgeting, financial reporting, pricing, staff supervision, and venue use analysis.[6]

Yet another related position is that of the *tour promoter* (also known as a *concert promoter*). These are the individuals responsible for "getting the show on the road!" They organize live concert events for performing on the road/tour. The tour promoter offers employment to artist(s) and negotiates the live performance contract. He or she must obtain the performance venue, price the event or tour, and possibly provide air, sea, or land transportation for the touring artist(s). The promoter must also *promote*! That means making sure bodies are in seats when the curtain goes up. This is achieved through every economical way possible: television/radio ads, outdoor advertising, social media, promotional/media kits, online ads, and so on.[7]

ACADEMIC PROGRAMS

It's a good idea to study arts administration to improve your chances of landing a great job in the field. A number of arts administration programs are available at colleges and universities in the United States and around the world. Some programs also offer certificate programs for practitioners already in the field to receive continuing education and professional development.

Arts programs are vital to the life of all communities and to society at large. Pursuing a job in arts administration is a noble endeavor, and the impact these organizations have on the quality of life of the countless people they touch is immeasurable.

NOTES

1. "The Arts in 1960s America," Encyclopedia.com, https://www.encyclopedia.com/history/encyclopedias-almanacs-transcripts-and-maps/arts-1960s-america.

2. "Young People's Concerts," Wikipedia, https://en.wikipedia.org/wiki/Young_People%27s_Concerts.

3. "Arts in 1960s America."

4. Nielsen, *2015 U.S. Music Year-End Report*, Nielsen.com, January 6, 2016, http://www.nielsen.com/us/en/insights/reports/2016/2015-music-us-year-end-report.html.

5. League of American Orchestras website, http://www.americanorchestras.org.

6. Michael Hannan, *The Australian Guide to Careers in Music*, Music Council of Australia (Sydney: University of New South Wales, 2003), 250.

7. "Tour Promoter," Wikipedia, https://en.wikipedia.org/wiki/Tour_promoter.

12

THE FINAL MIX

Getting It Done

The way to get started is to quit talking and get doing.

—Walt Disney

Walt Disney was a man who obviously followed his own advice, and in his own way, he changed the world. You too should be on a personal mission to change the world in as big, medium, or small a way as is possible for you . . . all with the sounds of music.

Our journey in this book is nearing its end, but your journey in the music business is just beginning. Or perhaps you're continuing your original music industry journey but with an unexpected detour or side trip for which you need fresh direction and planning. Or possibly you've decided to completely change directions or simply alter your course slightly. Regardless of where you are in your journey, there are certain guiding principles of success upon which you can depend to complement this road map as you travel the sometimes smooth and exciting, sometimes bumpy and treacherous road of today's music business. Those principles are woven throughout this book, but the biggest and most important step to success once you have defined your goals is to take the first step . . . no matter how big or small.

Bruce Springsteen once said about Elvis Presley: "It was like he came along and whispered some dream in everybody's ear. And somehow we all dreamed it."[1] A lot of people have had the dream of big success in the music business, especially once they're inspired by others. And while it's great to be motivated and inspired by others' success, we should always be ourselves. For when one's artistic motivation and inspiration meets

Fig 12.1.   Getting Started Now. *Illustration by Richard Duszczak*

with his or her own individuality, along with preparation and opportunity, good and exciting things can happen. In other words, dream big and don't be afraid to be who you are. As was stated in chapter 1 and is reprised here: "Know thyself." For when you truly know yourself at the deepest level possible, you are poised to build upon that foundation to refine your talents, pay the price of discipline and focus, and make a statement artistically (or help support those who are making their own statements). Then, as college professor William Lane said, you can "let the excellence of your work be your protest."[2] The music business (like other industries) is filled with a lot of cheap talk and pure noise. *Do work that is original, authentic, and well crafted, and it will cut through the massive world's clutter and speak for itself on your behalf.*

MAKE YOUR OWN ROAD MAP

This book is subtitled "A Guide for Aspiring Professionals," and indeed one of its main focuses is to present you with directions, information, and ideas for success. But the truth is that everyone must ultimately plot his or her own course for success, albeit hopefully using the tried-and-true principles and stories of success contained within this book (and others) to help you reach your destination.

There are many paths to success. Although I was interested in the music business beginning in my high school years, it wasn't until I was in my midtwenties that I decided once and for all that I was going to throw myself completely and wholeheartedly into landing a job in the music business, no matter what. There is a book that had a seismic impact on my plan and strategy for getting my first job in the music business, and I highly recommend that book to you: *What Color Is Your Parachute?* by Richard Nelson Bolles. This book will help you answer three very important questions as you fine-tune your personal road map to success: (1) What are your best and most enjoyed skills? (2) Where do you want to use those skills? (3) Who has the power to hire you?

Best and Most Enjoyed Skills

A person who wants to be a doctor may have the raw intelligence and skills but be very uncomfortable at the sight of blood. A person who passionately wants to be a singer may actually be a poor singer (and the only people telling him or her that he or she is a great singer are his or her parents). The doctor type has the needed talent but also a major impediment to success in that chosen profession; the singer type has no real talent but plenty of passion. Make sure the aspect of the music business in which you choose to pursue makes use of not only your best skills but also your most enjoyed ones.

For example, remember when you were a child or adolescent and became involved in something . . . such as playing the piano, singing, writing a script, or crunching numbers . . . when you seemed to lose all track of time? Time wasn't a concern. You were totally absorbed in what you were doing, either by yourself or with others. That's a clear clue that this activity is tapping into what is potentially one of your best and most enjoyed skills. Once you feel you have a sense of those skills, test them again and again (and have your competence verified by people other than your immediate family and circle of friends).

Where to Use Those Skills

Once you have determined your best and most enjoyed skills, where might you use them? This means what sort of geographic location, as well as what sort of organization. Do you like warm weather or cold? Pick companies that are based in that part of the world. Do you like working with a lot of people or a small, tight-knit team? Seek out companies accordingly. As a rule, smaller companies offer the best opportunities for advancement and also the opportunity to learn a broad range of things within the industry (since smaller companies often rely on fewer people to do a variety of things).

Who Has the Power to Hire You?

You can talk to the receptionist of your dream company ad nauseam, but he or she most likely does not have the power to hire you. However, don't dismiss the receptionist! Or anyone. In today's streamlined music business, even receptionists can have influence on the one(s) who have the power. First impressions are lasting, and you don't want anyone saying that in the waiting area you were impatient and rude but when you met the CEO you were *channing* (besides, that's no way to live). Bottom line: Work your way to the decision-maker who can hire you. And then when you get there, figure out what's keeping that person up at night. Every potential employer comes to work each day with a laundry list of challenges that are facing him or her, especially in today's more-than-ever competitive music industry. Employers aren't getting out of bed each day to find a way to give you a job. Your task is to figure out their greatest challenges and position yourself as the answer to those challenges.

You can uncover those challenges by talking to the receptionist or as many others at the company as possible to gently and strategically finding out those unique challenges that are facing the organization in which you want to work. Then come up with creative and fresh ways to help solve those challenges. If you can't discover those challenges prior to your meeting with the person who has the power to hire you, then ask that person point blank when the opportunity is given to you in your meeting with him or her. If nothing else, the person will be impressed that you're not thinking only about *you* . . . you are thinking about *the employer* and the company and how you can come in and earn your salary by *making a difference to the bottom line of that company*. Don't make the mistake many fresh-out-of-school college graduates make by going into an interview with an attitude of "Here's my diploma, now where's my job?" A sense of entitlement will turn off any potential employer. Your job is to position yourself as a problem solver. And of course, do your homework by visiting the company website before you set foot in the place.

HAVE A PLAN

In his book *How to Get Control of Your Time and Your Life*, personal time management expert Alan Lakein writes, "Planning is bringing the future into the present so that you can do something about it now."[3] A plan is different from a road map. A road map says "this is where I am and the path I am going to take to get me where I want to be." A plan is "this is how I'm going to get there" (e.g., a car, a bus, a jet). The streets of the music business are littered with people who said they were going to get to where they wanted to go but never got there because they didn't have a realistic strategy (or "vehicle") to get them there. Perhaps your plan/goal is to network enough so as to make connections with five companies in the next two months (more on networking later). Subsequently, your plan is to land interviews with at least three out of the five companies you originally targeted. Or if you are a songwriter, your plan is to write 10 new songs and get them on the desks of five music publishers in the next six weeks. Once you have those goals set, then your plan can take shape as far as how you go about meeting those goals.

Another logistical/practical aspect of any plan is how one will support oneself during the search process. My advice to beginners is to have enough money in savings to last for at least six months (or even a year) past graduation. The same is true for any individual who is seeking a change of career to get into the music business. If you have this sort of financial cushion, it affords you the time to land a job in the music business. Perhaps the newly graduated music business major gets a part-time job at a local mall to help pay the rent, while such a job will afford the graduate the time to actively seek and apply for jobs, pitch songs, and so on. Or someone wishing to change careers can press vacation time and weekends into service to research and apply for jobs. Ideally, the career changer won't quit an existing job to try to get into the music business. And in any situation, if possible try to live in one of the three major music business centers (New York, Nashville, Los Angeles) to get that job. If you're already living in one of these locations, your chances of going to an interview on a moment's notice are greatly improved. If that's not possible, Skype or FaceTime sessions are wonderful alternatives these days.

PAY THE PRICE

There are countless stories of music business legends who worked their way up to the top from the bottom. For example, Frances Preston, late music industry pioneer, obtained a job in 1958 in Nashville to open the Southern Regional office for BMI. She worked her way up to vice president by 1964, becoming the first woman corporate executive in Tennessee and the first full-time performing rights representative in the South. She raised the profile and brought new awareness to the region's culture and helped connect art with industry in the area. Accordingly, Ms. Preston's work helped Nashville become one of the most important centers for professional songwriting in the world. By 1985, she'd become senior vice president of BMI/Performing Rights. She became president and CEO the following year.[4]

Superstar singer/songwriter Taylor Swift wrote personal thank-you notes to the program directors of the radio stations who played her songs in the early days of her career. She probably doesn't have time to do that anymore, but she knew a genuine personal touch couldn't hurt her cause.

Legendary recording artist Barry Manilow got his start at CBS-TV while he was a student trying to make ends meet. Later, he studied musical theatre at the Juilliard performing arts school. Eventually, Manilow met a CBS director who gave him the assignment to arrange songs for an Off-Broadway musical. Instead, Manilow penned a completely original musical score for the show. The director ended up using Manilow's score, and the show had an amazing eight-year run. Manilow then transitioned to working as a pianist, producer, arranger, and eventually commercial jingle writer.[5] He went on to sell more than 75 million records worldwide, making him one of the world's best-selling artists of all time.[6]

TO GET A MUSIC BUSINESS DEGREE . . . OR NOT?

Frances Preston, Taylor Swift, Barry Manilow, and I have something in common (although I greatly flatter myself by even putting myself in the same sentence with those people): None of us has a degree in music business. So why get one? In the grand scheme of things, degrees in music business are still relatively new (unlike a degree in English or business administration, for example). But certainly, the area of music business education has made incredible advances in the last few decades, becoming a vital and, in my opinion, necessary path to success in today's music business. Still, the music industry is full of executives, managers, successful superstars, and others who don't have a degree in music business. But it's one of the best bets to give yourself the necessary knowledge and connections to be competitive in an extremely competitive business.

A college degree is your "license to learn." When you first sat in the driver's seat to learn how to drive a car, you had no experience on the road. But after you studied, obtained a learner's permit, did supervised practice driving with a professional, and then passed your state's prescribed examinations, you were granted a driver's license. But that didn't mean you were instantly a seasoned driver. It takes years of driving in actual conditions to become an experienced driver.

Such is the case with your college degree. Once you have taken and successfully passed all the prescribed courses, tests, and exams, you are awarded a degree. But that degree is a license to learn. Your real learning begins when you're "on the road" in the music business . . . doing it day after day, month after month, and year after year. You're paying the price to advance in the music business, just like Frances Preston, Taylor Swift, and Barry Manilow. Another maxim I share with music business students is: "Get your degree and get over it!" Just because you've earned a degree doesn't mean you're entitled to a job. Until you can prove your worth to a company, don't expect to be hired. Just because you receive a piece of paper, you don't instantly assume greatness or advanced wisdom. If you've developed good habits of professionalism throughout your college career (more on being a professional later), then when you graduate, the good habits of meeting deadlines, being disciplined, following instructions, presenting yourself well, and so on will be second nature, and you won't have to develop those skills on the job.

But what if you're fresh out of college with no real experience? Your grade point average can certainly help (if it's good, of course), but more important are glowing recommendations from former professors and any former employers where you did part-time work. Also, internships are a vital part of any music business program. So during your work for any organization as an intern, make sure you show up on time, follow instructions well, have a great attitude, and adopt the mind-set of "and then some." That means do everything you are asked, "and then some." Try not only to meet the expectations given to you but to exceed them.

Finally, "stretch" your degree. A rubber band is of no use until it's stretched. The same is true of a college degree. Leverage your college experience for all it's worth. Get your money's worth out of it (and then some!). Do this by obtaining internships and attending all seminars and lectures possible at your university. Seek your professors' advice before and after class on the topics about which you're passionate. Something I did often when I was in college (and beyond) was to seek out those people who were my heroes and try to interview them. Even (and sometimes especially) the busiest and most successful people will often take the time (30 minutes or an hour, for example) to meet with a college student to be interviewed for a student's paper. People generally love to talk about themselves and share their story. Even if a class doesn't require you to do an interview, do it anyway, and ask the professor if you might get extra credit for such a paper. Even if you don't get credit, do the interview and turn it in to your professor. The professor will be happy you took the initiative to do the interview and seek out one of your heroes. But most importantly, you'll have learned of a successful person's path in the music business and probably will have learned a lot that you can apply to your own game plan. And you will have made a wonderful connection, which can lead to more connections and networking.

NETWORK, NETWORK, NETWORK

One of my favorite lines in the movie *Superman* starring Christopher Reeve is when villain Lex Luthor (played by Gene Hackman) says to his stooge sidekick (played by Ned Beatty), "Some people can read *War and Peace* and come away thinking it's a simple adventure story. Others can read the ingredients on a chewing gum wrapper and unlock the secrets of the universe."

There can be opportunities that abound in one's life, but it takes someone who's willing and able to connect the dots. There's a way to seize opportunities in the music business without begin opportunistic. For example, someone with healthy and genuine enthusiasm (and good people skills) can network easily, and networking can open doors. One of the most common ways of networking is to join songwriting organizations such as the Nashville Songwriters Association International (NSAI), Global Songwriters Connection (GSC), West Coast Songwriters, songwriting "meet-up" groups, and so forth. Even if you're not a songwriter, you might consider attending one with a songwriting friend. These places are filled with experienced and novice songwriters alike, and the experienced ones generally have connections with record labels, music publishers, music business attorneys, and so on, which can lead to you networking your way to meeting people working where you would like to be. Meeting someone in person is always the best way to learn more and advance your career.

Again, however, always remember the rule of seeking first to help the other person before asking for help. Get to know that person as well as possible in the moment of networking and what is most important to them in their career at the time. You might be laying the foundation for a career-long friendship and professional association!

YES LIVES IN THE LAND OF NO

Legendary theatre impresario James L. Nederlander once said, "If they don't let you in the front door, go down the chimney." My personal definition of the path to success is "No, no, no, no, no, no . . . *yes*." Sometimes you have to get through a mountain of *nos* before you can get to a *yes*. And that *yes* may be the one that changes your life. Such was the case with my first published composition.

I had written many songs by the age of 26, but there was one song in particular I had written that year which I thought had really good market potential. So I packed it up and sent it off to a music publisher. I received a prompt rejection. Undaunted, I sent it off to publisher number two. Again, another rejection. I ended up sending the piece out to a few more publishers . . . and again, it was rejected. The piece then sat on my shelf for more than a year until finally, as the piece seemed to keep calling out to me, I gathered up my courage and sent it in to yet another publisher. And then one sunny afternoon, I received a phone call from that major music publisher in Nashville who asked, "May we have the pleasure of publishing your song?" It went on to be one of their best-selling releases that year. It has continued to sell for decades since then. But even more importantly, that same music publisher offered me my first job in the music business three years after they published my song. And that job led to the next, and that one to the next, and almost 30 years later, I'm still in the music business. That one *yes* to publish my song (after a list of *nos*) was the *yes* that launched my career. I call my home "the house that music built." And it all began with a single song.

YOU CAN'T HIDE TALENT

The music business is ultimately a small business. Sometimes it can seem as if everyone knows each other, even coast to coast. Those of us who have been in the business for years (and decades) celebrate and discuss the great leaders, great followers, and everyone in between in the industry. And the talented and nontalented alike are discussed.

You can't hide talent. The cream always rises to the top, as it's often said, and that's true in the music business as well. Therefore, if you get a job as a receptionist at a small record label, if you are doing an incredible job and have fabulous people skills, chances are you will be noticed by someone who's in a position to hire you tomorrow or next year. Or someone within your company is going to take notice of your talents and offer you a higher position with more money and bigger responsibilities to match. Likewise, if you have a poor attitude and do shabby work, that will follow you around as well. Get in the habit of being a professional, no matter what tasks you're assigned, and it will pay off either now or later.

BE A PROFESSIONAL

Being a professional in the music business—or any business, for that matter—is of paramount importance. I have known many people in the music business who made their living in it but they weren't professionals, in my opinion. Conversely, I have known people who didn't make a full-time living in the music industry but were consummate professionals. What made the difference? Here are my top 10 common denominators of true music business professionals:

10. *They don't miss deadlines.* The music business is full of deadlines, and these deadlines often can make or break a company. Of course, there are extenuating circumstances in many cases, but as a rule try never to miss deadlines when your company's depending on you.

9. *They're not afraid to ask "dumb" questions.* Not asking what might seem to you or others to be a "dumb" question shows that you might not be confident enough about your abilities. If you're confident in your abilities, you can ask dumb questions now and then. They are easier to handle than dumb mistakes.

8. *They're cheerful.* Leave any personal problems or concerns at the door when you enter each day. Strive to be cheerful in all circumstances. People don't always remember what you said to them, but they'll never forget how you made them feel.

7. *They're enthusiastic.* Enthusiasm is contagious. If you're genuinely excited about what you're doing or projects the company undertakes, that's going to go a long way in building up the company (or artist, songwriter, etc.) for which you work.

6. *They're punctual.* Simply put, being late is being inconsiderate. It can also be a control mechanism on the part of the person who is habitually late. Again, there are certainly extenuating circumstances to make a person late to a meeting or to work, but it should be an exception and not the rule.

5. *They do more than expected.* The "and then some" approach, as discussed earlier, clearly applies to being a professional.

4. *They're kind.* In the music business as in life, always strive to be kind. This includes consistently responding to emails and phone calls, even if it's a tardy response or a *no* to a request. You will encounter a variety of people in your music business career and not all will be milk and honey to deal with. Despite any sabotage you may receive along with way from a colleague, returning kindness will always trump revenge or unkindness. And just because you like someone doesn't mean you have to trust them in all things. Be watchful, be careful, be wise . . . but also be kind.

3. *They do excellent work.* Always. Excellence will triumph over mediocrity every time.

2. *They have integrity.* In all things great and small, this characteristic is priceless. Integrity can sometimes seem a precious commodity in the music business. One of the most famous quotes about the music business is from Hunter S. Thompson: "The music business is a cruel and shallow money trench, a long plastic hallway where thieves and pimps run free, and good men die like dogs. There's also a negative side."[7] While I don't completely agree with Thompson's quote, I do think there's a lot of truth in it. So, let there be integrity in the music business, and let it begin with you and me.

1. *They're grateful.* Making money making music is one of the best ways to make a living! Iconic game show host Bob Barker once told me, "I've never worked a day in my life." That's because he so loved what he did that it never felt as if he had to work for a living. That's the way the music business can be for those who love it. We should be grateful, not entitled, every day to make a living making music.

JUST DO IT!

I've attempted in this book to give you the essentials of the music business as a foundation for what I hope will be a lifelong and rewarding career for you. It's up to you to go out now and make it happen. It will not be easy, but the rewards can be both immediately and eventually very satisfying and beautiful. You can also make lifelong friends along the way, which is ultimately the best and most special aspect of any career in any industry. I am 100 percent convinced that when I come to the end of my career, I will say with complete honesty, "I would do it all over again." I hope you will too.

So now it's time to put your car in drive and enjoy the most exhilarating ride of your life!

NOTES

1. BrainyQuote.com, https://www.brainyquote.com.

2. Squinch.net, http://www.squinch.net.

3. Alan Lakein, *How to Get Control of Your Time and Your Life* (Hampshire, UK: Gower, 1995).

4. "Remembering Frances W. Preston," BMI, https://www.bmi.com/special/frances_preston.

5. "Barry Manilow," Wikipedia, https://en.wikipedia.org/wiki/Barry_Manilow.

6. BarryManilow.com, http://barrymanilow.com/.

7. "Hunter S Thompson: In His Own Words," *Guardian*, February 21, 2005, https://www.theguardian.com/books/2005/feb/21/huntersthompson.

GLOSSARY

360 deal. A business relationship between an artist and a music industry company wherein the company provides an "all-around" group of services. Marketing, promotion, touring, merchandising (or "merch"), and other areas of financial support are provided to the artist by the company in this type arrangement.

A&R (artists and repertoire). This division of a record label or music publisher scouts talent and oversees the artistic development of its songwriters and recording artists.

advance royalty. Money paid by record label or music publisher to a producer, artist, or songwriter in advance of actual earnings for a project(s) that person helped create and/or in which that person participated.

arranger. The person who formulates the musical setting for the notes and harmonies written by the composer.

artist. See **recording artist**.

artist management. Someone who negotiates contracts and fees; finds and books events and venues that match the artist's career strategy; advises on career choices, publicity, and promotion; assists the artist on career decisions such as which record producer to work with or which songs to perform; and manages media relations.

arts administration. This profession centers around the business mechanics (including funding) and regular operation around an arts organization, such as a symphony orchestra, ballet, theatre, or museum.

ASCAP. The American Society of Composers, Authors and Publishers is a nonprofit performing rights organization (PRO) that surveys public performances of songs, then collects and distributes directly to writers and publishers of those songs the monies that are due to them for those public performances.

Berne Convention. This international copyright–governing agreement was forged in Berne, Switzerland, in 1886. It mandated several aspects of modern copyright law and introduced the concept of a work being copyrighted the moment it is in a "fixed, tangible form." Before, registration of a work was the only legal way to copyright it.

BMI. Broadcast Music, Inc., is a nonprofit performing rights organization (PRO) that surveys public performances of songs, then collects and distributes directly to writers and publishers of those songs the monies that are due to them for those public performances.

Broadway. The Broadway Theatre (or simply "Broadway") consists of a group of theatres that seat 500 or more. There are currently 40 Broadway theatres located in the Theater District of Midtown Manhattan (including one in Lincoln Center).

business affairs. The department within a music business company that handles all contractual and legal matters.

business manager. This person handles and manages all business matters related to recording artists and musicians; that is, contract negotiations, investments, royalties, and so on.

CCLI (Christian Copyright Licensing International). Licensing organization founded in 1988 that serves as a blanket licensing organization for churches in their use of copyrighted music in worship.

clearance representative. Someone who works to negotiate and gain legal permission from the song's owner(s) to use a song or songs in television, film, etc.

combo retail store. Less broad in scope than a full-line music retail store, this store generally specializes in "combo" products: drums, guitars, amplifiers, speaker systems, audio mixers, public address systems, and lighting equipment, along with their accompanying accessories.

compulsory license. This provision of the copyright law provides that after a nondramatic musical work has been released in a first recording, the owner of that music is compelled by law to license any other person to produce and distribute recordings of the copyrighted music. In exchange, the copyright owner is entitled to receive the statutory mechanical rate as remuneration for such use.

concert venue manager. This person manages and is responsible for booking acts, managing employees, and all functions to assure the overall success of the venue. This includes cleanliness and equipment function.

contractor. See **music contractor**.

controlled compositions. Such songs are songs written, owned, or controlled by the artist. A controlled composition clause in a contract usually specifies that the record label won't pay more than 7.5 times the single-composition statutory rate for all cuts combined on an album, no matter how many are actually included.

Copyright Act of 1790. This act was the first federal copyright law to be enacted in the United States. Some states had previously passed various copyright legislation following the Revolutionary War, but this act codified copyright law coast to coast.

Copyright Act of 1909. Allowed for works to be copyrighted for a period of 28 years from the date of publication. A landmark statute in U.S. copyright law, it became public law on March 4, 1909.

Copyright Act of 1976. This act remains the primary basis of today's U.S. copyright law. It spelled out the basic rights of copyright holders and codified the doctrine of "fair use." It also adopted the unitary term based on the author's death rather than prior fixed and renewal terms. This law went into effect on January 1, 1978.

copyright assignment. The legal act of the original creator(s) of a work transferring and assigning the copyright of that work to another entity. This is accomplished through a written document (physical or electronic).

copyright infringement. The illegal use of works protected by copyright law.

copyright registration. The act of registering a copyright of a work with the United States Copyright Office.

Copyright Royalty Board (CRB). Consists of three copyright administrative royalty judges (appointed by the Librarian of Congress) who determine statutory license royalties.

cover version. A new performance recording or a previously recorded, commercially released song.

crossover. Term that applies to works or performers who appeal to additional audiences in addition to the originally intended one. For example, pop and country.

crowd funding. Funding a project or venture by raising small amounts of money from a large number of people, typically through the Internet.

cue sheet. See **music cue sheet**.

demo. A recording of a song or extended work intended to demonstrate the piece for prospective record labels, producers, or recording artists.

digital audio workstation (DAW). An electronic device or software application used for recording, editing, and producing audio files.

digital service provider (DSP). A company that provides an outlet to distribute media online.

executive producer. The person responsible for all business and financial decisions, hiring the producer, and ultimately accountable for the project's success or failure.

fair use. This is the legal doctrine stating that brief excerpts of copyrighted material may be used verbatim for purposes of criticism, news reporting, teaching, and research . . . without permission from or payment to the copyright owner.

full-line music retail store. A store that carries everything from pianos, guitars, band instruments, organs, orchestra, percussion, and printed music resources, as well as providing music lessons and classes.

Global Music Rights (GMR). A for-profit performance rights organization (PRO) in the United States.

grand rights. A term referring to stage performances of musical material within the context of a dramatic work.

Harry Fox Agency. Collector and distributor of mechanical license fees on behalf of music publishers in the United States. The agency also provides rights management services.

"indie" label. An independent record label that operates without support and/or funding from an outside record label.

J. W. Pepper. The world's largest printed music/music resources retailer.

League of American Orchestras. The North American musical organization network consisting of approximately 800 orchestral organizations.

Licensing of the Press Act 1662. An act of the Parliament of England intended to prevent "frequent abuses in printing seditious treasonable and unlicensed books and pamphlets and for regulating of printing and printing presses."

master recording. The original recording of the performance of a song or other musical work. Can be made on discs, tapes, computer data storage, and so on.

mechanical license. This license grants certain limited permissions to record a song in exchange for remuneration to the copyright holder.

mixing engineer (or **mix engineer**). The person responsible for combining ("mixing") the differing sounds/elements of a piece of recorded music into a final, mixed version.

music contractor. Someone who is a bit of a music "matchmaker." He or she has the job of finding the appropriate musicians for recording sessions for records, film, television, etc. Also acts as a liaison between the contracted musicians and the musicians' union to ensure proper pay and working conditions.

music cue sheet (or **cue sheets**). Log sheets that document all the music used in a production or broadcast. These sheets are the primary means by which performing rights organizations track music use and pay accordingly.

music director. Someone who is responsible for the musical aspects of a performance, production, or organization, typically the conductor or leader of a music group.

music production library. The repository for production music.

music promotion. The process of marketing and advertising music products and songs in order for them to achieve sales.

music publisher. A company responsible for the positive exploitation of its own copyrights, while ensuring that the songwriters and composers within their publishing catalog are remunerated when their compositions are used commercially or noncommercially.

music retailer. A store that sells musical instruments, accessories, and other music-related merchandise.

music supervisor. The person who oversees all music-related aspects of film, television, advertising, video games, theatre, and so on.

name/image/likeness (NIL). A royalty paid to a person(s) (or estate, if the person is deceased) in exchange for the use of that person's name, image, or likeness for the promotion of a product(s).

Napster. The original "file sharing" application that allowed its users to share music over the Internet without the need to purchase their own copy of the shared recording.

National Association of Music Merchants (NAMM). An international retail association to strengthen music retailers around the world. The organization also includes distributors and manufacturers.

National Foundation on the Arts and Humanities Act of 1965. An act of Congress that established the National Foundation on the Arts and Humanities to promote progress and scholarship in the humanities and the arts in the United States.

National Music Publishers Association (NMPA). Founded in 1917, this trade association for the American music publishing industry exists to protect its members' intellectual property rights in legislative, litigation, and regulatory areas.

Off-Broadway. Professional theatres in New York City with a seating capacity of 100–499. Unlike Broadway theatres, which are larger and located in the Theater District of New York City, Off-Broadway theatres are scattered throughout Manhattan.

online music store. Web-based retailer that sells copyrighted songs and albums in physical and/or digital format for a fee.

orchestrator. Someone who artistically chooses which instrument plays what in a song while keeping in mind the technical capabilities of each orchestral instrument. Orchestrators also often add their own original musical motifs and countermelodies to complement the existing musical score.

performing rights organization (PRO). Organizations that collect money from users of qualifying public music performances and distribute those royalties to the copyright holders/songwriters of the surveyed songs. Also known as performing rights societies.

personal manager. Person who focuses on overall career advancement for the artist(s) he or she manages.

PR (public relations) agency. A professional services organization generally hired to conceive, produce, and manage unpaid messages to the public through the media on behalf of a client, with the intention of shaping and/or changing the public's perceptions and/or actions by influencing their opinions.

print license. A license obtained by a commercial or noncommercial entity that wishes to use copyrighted materials (e.g., music and/or lyrics) in printed format (e.g., a songbook, printed program, greeting card).

producer. Person who oversees and manages the sound recording and production of an artist's or band's recording and/or live performances. For a recording, a producer helps gather ideas for the project, assists the artist(s) to fine-tune the content, supervises the actual recording, and assures the project stays on budget and is delivered to the record label on time.

production ("stock") music. Recorded music licensed to customers for use in film, television, radio, and other media. Often such music is offered on a lump-sum payment basis versus a royalty usage.

professional musician. A singer, instrumentalist, or other musically talented person who is paid to use that talent on a part-time or full-time basis.

publicist. The person whose job it is to generate and manage publicity for an artist, band, or other celebrity.

radio plugger. Also known as a radio promoter. This person or firm is charged with the responsibility of getting the artist, band, or record label's music played on the radio as frequently as possible.

Recording Academy. An American-based organization of musicians, producers, recording engineers, and other recording professionals; presents the Grammy Awards annually.

recording artist. A person who performs music for recordings.

recording engineer (or **audio engineer**). The person who acts as the technical supervisor of a recording project under the direction of the producer. The engineer handles all technical aspects of the recording: selecting appropriate microphones, physical placement of the musicians in the session, adjusting sound levels during the recording process, troubleshooting, and so on.

school music store. A store that specializes in serving school music programs by providing music (choral, band, orchestra, jazz, solo, etc.) geared toward directors and students. Printed music and lessons are prominent in such stores, although music products such as pianos and guitars are sometimes carried.

SESAC. American for-profit performing rights organization (PRO) that surveys public performances of songs, then collects and distributes directly to writers and publishers of those songs the monies that are due to them for those public performances. Originally founded as the Society of European Stage Authors and Composers, it is now known exclusively as SESAC.

small rights. Rights obtained for music not especially written for a dramatic presentation (see also **grand rights**).

song exploitation. The promotion and exposure of a song for commercial purposes to achieve revenue.

song plugger (or **song demonstrator**). The person who pitches songs to potential users of those songs: producers, A&R reps, managers, artists, music supervisors, and so on.

sound recordings. An analog or digital album or single re-creation of a performance, such as singing, instrumental music, spoken voice, and so on.

SoundScan. Data collection service that tallies sales of recorded products through POS (point of sale) devices.

special products. Products produced by or produced in participation with record labels or music publishers that reach specialized markets, such as film, television, and unique licensing opportunities (such as toys).

specialty music shop. A store that specializes in one or only a few music products, such as guitars or pianos.

Statute of Anne. An act of the Parliament of Great Britain (also known as the Copyright Act of 1710). This act was the first statute to provide for copyright regulated by the government and courts rather than by private parties.

studio musician (or **session musician/backing musician**). Instrumentalist employed to perform in a recording session (or live performance). Usually paid union scale.

synchronization (or **"sync"**) **license**. The right granted by a copyright holder to the user to use licensed music in such a way that it is timed to synchronize with action on film or video.

talent agency. An agency that specializes in the booking of talent such as in music, broadcasting, film, television, and/or modeling.

Tin Pan Alley. The area in New York City (West 28th Street between Fifth and Sixth Avenues) given to a collection of music publishers of the day (late 19th and early 20th century). After many years, the term came to occasionally refer to the U.S. music industry in general.

tour promoter (or **concert promoter** or **talent buyer**). The person or company responsible for organizing and promoting a live concert, tour, or special event performance.

Universal Copyright Convention. One of two principal international conventions that protect copyright (the other being the Berne Convention). Adopted in Geneva, Switzerland, in 1952.

INDEX

ABOUT THE AUTHOR

Mark Cabaniss is a music publisher, writer, producer, educator, and broadcaster. He is president/CEO of Jubilate Music Group and also serves as an adjunct professor of music business at Belmont University. Mark's published songs and musicals have been performed throughout the United States and abroad. He is a multiple recipient of ASCAP's Popular Music Award and NAMM's Believe in Music Award and is also a Dove award–winning producer. He is a member of the Recording Academy and the Dramatists Guild. Mark is also a correspondent for the nationally syndicated radio show *Hollywood 360*. He serves on the board of advisors for the Music Man Square, a museum and foundation in Mason City, Iowa, dedicated to furthering music education and honoring the legacy of Meredith Willson (creator of Broadway's *The Music Man*). Mark was named Outstanding Alumnus of the Year by Mars Hill University and serves on the university's board of trustees. He is also the founder/donor of the Helen Cole Krause Music Scholarship, awarded annually to qualifying students. His work in the music business and broadcasting has included collaborations with Bob Barker, Kathie Lee Gifford, Charles Strouse, David Pomeranz, Steve Allen, Rupert Holmes, Andy Griffith, and more. He holds bachelor's and master's degrees in music education and communications from Mars Hill University and the University of Tennessee–Knoxville. Mark resides in Nashville, Tennessee. www.markcabaniss.com.